Feathers of the Skylark

Compulsion, Sin and Our Need for a Messiah

AF853492

A HAMEWITH BOOK

Jeffrey B. Satinover, MD

Hamewith Books
Post Office Box 5191
Westport, Connecticut 06881

Cover design © YbJ Artworks

This work is subject to copyright. All rights are reserved whether the whole or part of the material is concerned, specifically the rights of translation, reprinting, reuse of illustrations, recitation, broadcasting, reproduction on microfilm or any other way, and storage in databanks. Duplication of this publication or of parts thereof is permitted only under the provisions of the United States Copyright Law in its current version and permission for use must always be obtained from Hamewith Books, Ltd. Violations are liable for prosecution under The United States Copyright Law.

© Hamewith Books, 1996

The use of general descriptive names, registered names, trademarks, etc., in this publication does not imply, even in the absence of a specific statement, that such names are exempt from the relevant protective laws and regulations and therefore free for general use. Certain material herein used with permission from *Homosexuality and the Politics of Truth* by Jeffrey Satinover, Baker Book House Company, ©1996 by Jeffrey Satinover.

Designed, copy-edited and typeset
by Beinoni, SP, Westport, Connecticut

ISBN 0-9652945-0-1

Jeffrey Satinover, MD

Feathers of the Skylark:
Compulsion, Sin and Our Need for a Messiah

Hamewith Books
Westport, Connecticut

For Annie...

...and for all those whose sensitivity and giftedness directs them to a higher calling than they themselves know. To the 1995 Wheaton PCM school: my heartfelt thanks. It was you—Leanne Payne, team members and participants—who encouraged me in the writing of this book.

My special thanks to Rabbi Yehoshua Hecht of Beth Israel Synagogue in Westport, Connecticut, for your friendship and counsel—and for directing me to the *Likutei Amarim* of Schneur Zalman, the *Alter Rebbe.* What will that day look like when Jews and Christians each understand the treasures of the other? I speculate, but tremble to say. Hints reside herein.

I am most grateful to Ruth Goring for her fine editing of the manuscript.

אלא אפילו מי שהוא בעל עסקים ודרך ארץ אם נופל לו
עצב ודאגה ממילי דשמיא בשעת עסקיו בידוע שהוא תחבולת
היצר כדי להפילו אחר כך בתאוות חס ושלום כנודע

"Should a sense of failure, even over spiritual matters, descend upon you, it is but a snare. For the Evil One knows full well that thereby you will later succumb to temptation."

Part One

Unattainable Longings

Man's reach must exceed his grasp;
Else what's a heaven for?

—Robert Browning

Remembering Heaven

An ancient Jewish legend tells of *HaGuf*, "the well of souls." This is the place of waiting for all the souls that will ever be born, from Adam to the end of time. As they wait, they are instructed by angels in all the matters of Heaven. But just before the time comes for a particular soul to begin its earthly sojourn, an angel touches it above the lips, and it forgets all that it has been taught.

And so it is that throughout our lives we recall only a faint impression of Heaven—like the small indentation we bear on our upper lip. Yet whether we realize it or not, it is this dimly perceived vision—and the longing it stirs deep within us—that drives us on through life. We are lonely for Heaven.

I once heard a lovely story that reminded me of this legend of the well of souls. A young couple came home from the hospital with their newborn baby girl. The moment they walked in the door, her sister, four years old, began clamoring to see her and touch her. But the parents were a bit nervous about the older daughter's importuning; they had heard that older siblings were sometimes jealous of little usurpers and, being too young to deal with their anger in less destructive ways, would at times hurt the upstart. (I indeed recall being told many times how when my own younger brother arrived—I was the oldest—I tried pulling his legs through the bars of his crib in all too Freudian a fashion.)

After the little baby was placed in her crib in a nursery, the four-year-old kept begging to be allowed to visit her—alone. Finally the parents agreed. Since they had placed an intercom in the baby's room, they reasoned that they could listen in, ready to intervene should the interaction take a bad turn. Letting their older daughter walk into the room and close the door, they turned up the monitor and listened.

This is what they heard: their daughter rushed over to the crib and whispered urgently, "Hurry! Tell me about Heaven; I'm beginning to forget!"

When we allow ourselves to sense it (and for many, this is not necessarily often), we realize that our longing for Heaven, for goodness, and for God is profound indeed. Mostly we deny its existence, or divert it into other, idolatrous aims (if we cannot really be good, why then we shall be good-looking, or rich, or famous, or sexy). But at heart, everyone struggles—knowingly or not—to conform to an image of holiness that was planted deep within our hearts at the moment our souls were created. We know it is there because of the exquisite, painful, even tearful tenderness that overcomes us whenever we are confronted with acts of genuine virtue: the man who lays down his life for another; the restoration of long-broken bonds of love;

the reconciliation of mortal enemies in peace and genuine understanding.

We long to be close to God and to be something like him. Yet our sense of distance from him, our painful awareness of just how unlike him we are, leads us to fling ourselves desperately into innumerable distractions.

Forgetting Heaven

Our forgetfulness of Heaven, and of our place in it, is part of the mystery of being born into a fallen world. We are all Adams and Eves, looking back over our shoulder at what we have lost even as we are driven ever further from it. But we also participate willfully in this forgetting, removing ourselves ever further from the divine image. We do this via *sin*.

Many of us tend to think of sin simply as acts that are morally wrong—and it is that. But sin is more than that: it is a distinct kind of process as well, one with a predictable, internal dynamic of its own, and with inevitable consequences. The writer of Proverbs put it this way:

> The evil deeds of a wicked man ensnare him;
> the cords of his sin hold him fast.
> He will die for lack of discipline, led astray by
> his own great folly. (Proverbs 5:22-23)

In like vein, the prophet Isaiah warned:

> Woe to those who draw sin along with cords
> of deceit,
> and wickedness as with cart ropes. (5:18)

Later, in the Talmud (the Jewish interpretation and expansion of the Hebrew Scriptures), Rabbi Assi interpreted this remark of Isaiah as follows: "The Evil Inclination is at first like the thread of a spider, but ultimately becomes like cart ropes" (Sukkah 52a). And Rabbi Isaac stated: "The Evil Inclination of a man grows stronger within him from day to day, as it is said, 'Only evil all the day.'"

Taking it one step further, Rabbi Simeon ben Lakish stated, "The Evil Inclination of a man grows in strength from day to day and seeks to kill him, as it is said, 'The wicked watcheth the righteous and seeketh to slay him ... '"

But Rabbi Isaac, in another interpretative text, put it most pointedly: "At first, sin is like an occasional visitor, then like a guest who stays for awhile, and finally like the master of the house."[1]

What the inspired writers and prophets of the Scriptures are saying, along with their later commentators, is that sin is not simply "wrong," it is invariably progressive as well, attracting and ensnaring us in ever-deepening moral incapacitation. Sin, in short, not only represents a simple momentary failure of the will but progressively weakens and undermines the will, eventually destroying it altogether. Sin is rather like addiction; for compulsion is central to it.

The Tale of the Skylark

The following fable illustrates the journey by which people become ensnared in compulsive behavior.

One day long ago, over the hot sands of a Middle Eastern country, a white skylark flew in joyous loops about the sky. As she swooped near the earth, she heard a merchant cry out, "Worms! Worms! Worms for feathers! Delicious worms!"

The skylark circled about the merchant, hungry at the mention of worms but puzzled as to what the merchant meant. Little did the skylark know that the merchant was the devil. And seeing that the little skylark was interested, the devil motioned her nearer. "Come here, my little friend. Come! See the lovely worms I have!"

Cautiously, the skylark landed and cocked her head at the merchant. "Come! Taste the juicy worms!" The skylark became aware that she was indeed quite hungry. And these worms looked bigger and tastier than any she had ever dug for herself out of the hardscrabble ground of the desert. The skylark hopped closer and put her beak up close to a worm. "Two worms for a feather, my friend. Two worms for one!"

The skylark was unable to resist. And she had, after all, so many feathers. So, with a swift motion, she pulled out a feather—just a small one—from beneath her wing and gave it to the merchant. "Take your pick, my little friend ... any two, your heart's desire!" And so the skylark quickly snatched up two of the plumpest worms and swallowed her meal with delight. Never before had she tasted such wonderful worms. With a loud chirp, she leaped into the air and resumed her joyful flight.

Day after the day the skylark returned. And always the merchant had wonderful worms to offer: black ones and blue ones, red ones and green ones, all fat and shiny and iridescent.

But one day, after eating her fill, the skylark leaped again into the air—and to her horror, she fell to the ground with a thud. She was unable to fly!

All at once, with a shock, she realized what had happened. From the delicious worms she had grown fatter and fatter; and as she plucked her feathers one by one, first her body, then her tail, and finally her very wings had grown balder and balder.

Horrified, she remembered how, slowly, imperceptibly, day by day, it had been getting harder and harder to fly; and how she had told herself it was no matter; she could always stop before it was too late. Now, suddenly, here she was, trapped on the ground. She looked up and saw the merchant looking at her. Was that a small, sly grin spreading across his face?

In terror, the skylark ran off into the desert. She ran and ran and ran and ran. It took her hours and hours. Never in her entire life had she walked or run so far. Finally she came to the softer ground near the desert springs where, before she met the merchant, she daily had come to dig for herself the small, dusty brown desert worms that could be found around the springs.

The skylark dug and dug in a frenzy. She piled up worm after worm until it was nearly dark. Then, wrapping her catch in a small fallen palm frond, she dragged it off back across the sand to where she saw the merchant closing up his stall for the night.

The skin around her beak had grown bruised and tender; her small feet were bleeding from the great distances she had been forced to walk. "Oh, merchant! Oh, merchant! Please help me! Please help me! I cannot fly anymore! Oh, dear what shall I do? Please, please, take these worms from me and give me back my feathers!"

The merchant bent down and peered at the terrified skylark. He threw back his head and roared with laughter, a gold tooth glinting in the red and setting sunlight. "Oh, I'll take those worms all right, my friend. A few weeks in this good soil and they, too, will be fat and green and glistening." He unwrapped the worms and tossed them into a jar of black and humid soil.

"But feathers?" He laughed again. "What will you do with feathers? Glue them on with spit?" He wheezed and cackled at his little joke.

"Besides, my friend"—the merchant reached down and grabbed the already plucked and fattened skylark—"that's not my business: 'feathers for worms.' Oh no!" He threw the skylark into a cage. "My business is 'worms for feathers!'" The merchant slammed the little cage door shut and smiled hungrily at his victim, and with a loud SNAP! of his fingers, he vanished into the desert air.

As our fable tells us, each time we behave in a certain way—each time the skylark exchanges a feather for worms—there is an important sense in which we choose to do so. And each time we do, we tell ourselves the truth that we are free to choose not to. Yet it is also true that with each successive step we progressively lose the ability to turn around, and yet are unaware of this worsening, insidious moral incapacitation. This is the devil's bargain we make with each successive step we take. At the end, it seems we are completely trapped, and can no more undo the subtle effects we have allowed to develop within us (as we will discuss shortly, these are actual changes in the brain) than the leopard can change his spots, or the skylark buy back her feathers. From this trap there may eventually become no escape—none, that is, without the help of God.

The story of the skylark, which is based on a Jewish and Christian view of reality, also tells us something quite specific and important about who we are: we were not meant to spend our lives pursuing shiny worms, however glistening or brilliant; we were meant to fly (we are in fact citizens of Heaven). Thus there is a special poignancy to the fate of those who have become trapped in sinful ways of life, and a special wonder in the stories of those who have gained freedom.[2]

To use an example which is now widely misunderstood and distorted in popular opinion, the many people (not few, as media-influenced opinion has it) who have successfully left the so-called gay lifestyle have done so with great difficulty not because homosexuality is inborn (as is now commonly misrepresented) but because typical homosexual behavior is very compelling—more precisely, compulsive. (As we will discuss shortly, all forms of illicit sexuality are compulsive.)

Compulsive behaviors are very difficult, at times seemingly impossible, to change—so much so that people find themselves doing things, over and over, and quite irrationally, for which they pay an extremely high personal cost—even death. This is nowhere more readily seen than in the enormous dangers to which homosexual men continue to expose themselves, in spite of many years of efforts to encourage and teach them to change their practices (not, however, to seek change in the basic problem itself).[3] Indeed, so fruitless have been these efforts that a new literature is now arising—in respectable journals of sexuality—aimed at justifying fatal behavior on the grounds that the sexual satisfaction it offers is worth the price.[4]

Whether the compulsion is to dangerous sex, or adultery and philandering, or gambling or stealing or drugs or food—any misused and abused source of pleasure—it characteristically persists in the face of self-destruction, even to the point of death. Anyone who has tried to use rational arguments to get a friend to stop, say, smoking or drinking, has seen this first-hand. It is indeed the case that "the cords of his sin hold him fast" and that eventually he truly "will die for lack of discipline, led astray by his own great folly."

In any discussion of sinful behavior—especially when discussing change in such behavior (and this may be seen especially clearly today in the debate over homosexuality, but it applies in any instance)—confusion arises from an imprecise use of the term choice as applied to habitual behavior that eventually becomes compulsive. Habit has an explicit biological basis in the brain (for which the skylark's feathers provide a nice analogy), but this biological connection is different from, say, genetics or prenatal influences. Once we understand the biology of habit (a subject we will take up shortly), we will also have a better understanding of why habits, compulsions, and addictions are so resistant to change—yet not impossibly so.

Part Two

The Search for a Pain-Free Existence

The Flight from Pain

THERE IS ANOTHER important dimension to understand about sin, one that follows directly when we have grasped the fact that the behaviors named in Scripture as sinful are also compulsive. This is the additional fact that *compulsive sinning arises from our attempts to relieve distress.*

This is how it happens: Adam and Eve are driven from Eden. In their pain—not just their grief but also the realities of their new, fallen natures (having now to struggle for existence and suffer the pain of bringing the next generation into the world)—they look back longingly. But having been driven from the direct presence of God, the greatest solace, they fail to turn their eyes up to the Creator and instead bend downward, abusing the creation to soothe their aching souls. Thus they compound the first and ancient sin with another and another.

Of course there is nothing wrong with attempting to relieve distress. Indeed, we are specifically designed to do so. Pain is purposeful, meant to alert us to take action to escape something dangerous to our physical, emotional or spiritual well-being. Yet everything hinges on the nature of the action we take.

If I place my hand in a fire, it burns and hurts badly. The safe and effective response to this pain, obviously, is to remove my hand. But an equally effective—in fact more effective—method of relieving the pain would be to kill it entirely, say by taking high doses of pain-killing drugs or severing the responsible nerves. But such an action is hardly safe. It is, rather, very risky. For from that point on I could "safely" place my hand in the fire without any pain at all.

Note the rather obvious point that the word safe is being used ironically: what feels good (as though safe) is actually bad (greatly dangerous).

The Causes of Emotional Pain

There are many different kinds of distress to which we are painfully subject. This discussion, however, is not so much concerned with overtly physical distress, such as burning one's hand in a flame. We are more concerned with emotional pain. But even emotional pain has many different sources. These may be conveniently divided into four main categories: psychological, biological, symbolic and spiritual.

Psychological Distress: The Effect of Nurture

Of the many causes of psychological distress, certainly the major one derives from the disappointments and hurts that inevitably occur in family life, when the needs of a tender young child are not adequately met by his parents. Of course, there are many reasons this happens. Some parental failures are simply the inevitable consequence of living in a less-than-perfect world; others are dire and malignant, such as when a parent truly hates or abuses a child.

But one important, overarching point needs to be made here: parents need not be particularly "bad" in order for bad effects to occur. Intense emotional distress can come merely because the abilities and habits of a parent—however normal and lovingly intended and consensually reasonable they may be—happen not to fit well with the particular needs of a child.

Children are not clones of their parents. Each of us comes into the world with our own distinctive set of dispositions and needs. Given that reality, it is quite possible that a decent, well-intentioned parent who behaves in accordance with generally accepted standards of goodness may nevertheless be unable to offer a child precisely what he or she needs. (The very same approach may, on the other hand, suit to a T another child in the family whose dispositions and needs happen to mesh more closely with those of his parents.)

While in no way denying the adverse effects and truly sinful nature of genuinely harsh or disinterested parents, this point reminds us that psychological distress is always subjective. It is not the objective behavior of others toward us which is the final arbiter, as it were, of distress, but rather our own experience of and response to that behavior. Some children do surprisingly well in quite harsh environments; others do surprisingly poorly in what most outside observers would agree is a quite decent one. What may be harshly damaging—and taken in as a grievous sin—to the sensitive child, may be a matter of relative indifference to one with an "alligator hide." For example, while I do not think I have ever met a child known to have been sexually molested who has not suffered from the experience, I have met many whose wounding has been relatively minor, and many others, of course, for whom the wounding has been major indeed.

God has his own standards of judging sinfulness. Only he can look into the heart and know the relative degrees of culpability and innocence within any person. We are naturally tempted to form our own judgments about others based on the presumption that their degree of culpability is directly proportional to our own distress. But this is not necessarily—or at least, not perfectly—so.

The reason for emphasizing this variability in subjective responsiveness is because of how directly it relates to the next source of emotional pain, biological distress.

Biological Distress: The Effect of Nature

At least one of the major factors that cause different children to react differently to the same stress is temperament. And one of the most important dimensions of temperament is the tendency to anxiety. With respect to one's vulnerability to later problems in life—

especially the disposition to fall into compulsive "self-soothing" of one sort or another—this is the most important factor. Although many other traits interweave with it, it is the degree to which one responds with anxiety to any given stress that determines one's "sensitivity."

In reality, "sensitivity" is likely to consist of many different elements, only one of which could fairly be called a "heightened anxiety response." Still, anxiety is certainly one of the most important quantifiable components of sensitivity, and it brings both benefits and costs.

In social situations, for example, the more sensitive person is likely to detect subtle currents of distress that less sensitive people may miss. An excellent hostess is likely to be exquisitely sensitive to subtle indicators of distress in others—which produces tension within herself—and thus is able to respond quickly and effectively to others' needs. On the other hand, she is also more likely to suffer at length when things go wrong. If she is "too" sensitive, the cost of her "gift" may in time exceed its benefits, and she may avoid such social responsibilities entirely. (Our English word gift, incidentally, is cognate to the German *Gift*, meaning "poison.")

When a "nervous" hostess feels she must perform social obligations despite her anxieties, she may deal with her sensitivity by having some alcohol beforehand—the most widely used, and abused, method of self-soothing.

This scenario happens also to shed light on one of the most commonly misunderstood aspects of the genetics of behavior. For many years researchers had noticed that alcoholism seemed to "run in families." Did this mean that alcoholism was genetic and could be inherited? Some researchers thought so, and they set off on a search to find the "alcohol gene." But no such gene turned up. The researchers discovered that alcoholism itself is not inherited at all. Rather, an intense anxiety response is inherited, and people with such an intense response find their way more readily into alcohol use and abuse—because it does so much more for their "nerves" than for the person who tends to stay pretty calm anyway.

In other words, although alcoholism is (to a certain degree) heritable, it is not directly inherited: there is no gene for alcoholism, but rather for an intermediate trait (anxiety) that makes alcoholism more likely. (The same is true, by the way, for supposed genetic findings regarding homosexuality. There is no such thing as "the gay gene" or genes.) And this should not surprise us: after all, why should we have developed a genetic predisposition for something so unhelpful as alcoholism?

So our biological predisposition to low versus high anxiety interacts with the circumstances of life to produce what we subjectively experience as less or more distress. This means that the sinful responses we all have to such states of distress cannot be judged superficially. There may be mitigating facts of inherited temperament quite invisible to us.

This principle is perhaps easiest to see when we turn it the other way around: we all greatly admire those who, with the help of God, have struggled successfully to emerge from lifestyles of great sinfulness—let us once again use the example of homosexuality. But how much credit do we give the person who never has indulged this particular sin—because he's never been tempted? It is really quite easy, after all, to avoid the besetting sins of others!

Symbolic Distress

There is yet one more subtlety regarding distress that we must consider briefly: because of the peculiar and amazing nature of the human mind, we are inevitably subject to distress that may be not just individualized (because of each person's unique temperament and upbringing) but also purely symbolic, most commonly communicated by language and woven into the fabric of our mental representation of life.

We do not react so much to the objective intensity of a stressor (say, as measured on some scale) as we do to our subjective perception of it. This kind of subjective difference among people is distinct from our predisposition to react moderately or intensely to any given situation-as-perceived. In other words, some situations are perceived as very distressing by some people, but hardly at all by others; to this subjective sense of degree of danger, as it were, there is then added the question of how intensely one reacts to it.

Here is an example. Imagine that I set a long, heavy wooden plank—say six inches wide and ten feet long—on the ground. Now I ask you to walk on the board from one end to the other. Assuming that you are physically healthy, sober, and willing, this task will probably cause you no anxiety. It really isn't threatening at all, neither to your physical well-being nor to your sense of self (unless you *are* drunk, and I am a policeman who has pulled you over).

Now let's make the task a shade more difficult. This time I blindfold you and ask you to "walk the plank" again. You agree, because this time, again, the task isn't really all that hard, dangerous, or otherwise threatening.

To raise the ante just a bit, let's say we make a bet: I bet you fifty dollars that you can't make it from one end to the other without stepping off the board. Now, perhaps, your heart beats a bit faster, and your palms are just a tad moist—because something is riding on your success: fifty dollars, a moderately meaningful amount of money.

Still, you experience only the very slightest sense of threat—not enough to prevent you from trying. And chances are you'll win the bet. As you walk, instead of looking at the board's edges (which now you can't see), you feel them carefully with your feet. You need therefore to proceed more cautiously, but still there is little fear.

Now, after you've accomplished this task with alacrity and won your fifty dollars, I ask if you'd like to win $100,000 for doing exactly the same thing. You're suspicious, of course, but curious. I refuse to explain further, except to say that the next task is absolutely no different from the one you've just finished. You must walk an identical ten-foot-long, six-inch-wide plank from end to end, blindfolded, without stumbling or falling; and if you do, you win $100,000. If you fail, you owe me nothing. You may back out at any point without penalty. So, after numerous assurances that you have nothing to lose, you agree.

Keeping you blindfolded, I walk you along a corridor to an elevator. You feel the elevator ascend for quite a long time. At length we emerge and walk to another door, which you hear me unlock. As I open the door, you feel a gust of wind and hear distant traffic noises. Suddenly, your heart starts racing, and your palms begin sweating in earnest. "Wait a minute," you think. "What's going on here?"

I give you a gentle nudge in the small of your back, and as you resist by leaning backward and digging in your heels just slightly, your left foot touches the end of the plank. Your heart leaps into your throat. "No way!" you cry out.

As you back away into me, you tear off the blindfold angrily. "How could he put me in such danger," you think, "for any amount of money?" Your thought is cut off in mid-high-dudgeon, however, for standing in front of you, in a regular room, at the other end of the plank—which is resting on the floor—is a small group of laughing people, one of whom is tearing into little pieces what surely looks like a check. A large fan is blowing irregular gusts of air at you, and from a loudspeaker come the sounds of distant traffic, probably recorded out of doors in New York City.

What made you afraid? Not the actual danger, but the perceived danger. Your entire symbol system, encoded in your brain over a lifetime, created for you a mental image of a threatening reality that was in fact not real at all.

And this story in reverse would make the same point. Were you adequately convinced—by the symbols you held in your mind—that the plank was indeed once again lying on the floor, you'd have been perfectly willing to walk it again, even if in reality it was suspended hundreds of feet above the ground.

We react with a sense of fear to what our symbol system tells us is dangerous. While most times this symbol system is in fact closely coupled to reality, many times it isn't. And our symbol system's correspondence to reality is very fluid indeed when we are dealing with emotional and spiritual reality—symbols that mediate our sense of being and worth.

Most of the subjective differences among our perceptions of what is threatening and what is not lie in the domain of the symbolic. These kinds of symbolic threats do not directly affect our physical well-being so much as our sense of ourselves (in particular, our vanity) and of our place in a larger scheme of things (if our symbol system even allows for such a thing; many modernist systems do not).

If you are convinced that the earthly "vale of tears" is only temporary, that beyond all earthly vanities your truest identity is to be a child of God, that you can look ahead eagerly to the day, not far off, when you will return to Heaven forever, you will have very little indeed to fear in this life among your fellow human beings.

(Remembering the very last scenario above, where you imagined safety in a situation of danger, you may of course wonder if such beliefs are nothing but comforting illusions. But that would imply we are passing strange creatures—miscreants, really: beings who achieve their highest capacities, fulfill their deepest longings, and attain their greatest nobility of character only when completely deluded!)

Spiritual Distress

There is one last and most important area of distress that we must address briefly now (and in greater detail later): spiritual distress. Though human beings are quite different from animals simply in their degree of use of symbols, the greatest difference between people and all other creatures is *our need for higher meaning* in life. And the symbols that mediate this higher meaning are the very most significant to us, far more important in the long run than the ones we use to navigate our day-to-day affairs.

Over the centuries, out of our symbolizing capacity we human beings have produced vast amounts of literature, and the great bulk of this literature is devoted to this question of life's meaning. Directly and indirectly "What is the meaning of life?" is asked in thousands of different ways. Some of our literature proposes answers; even more of it discusses and debates and elucidates those answers. Some of it goes to great lengths to argue that there is no way of knowing the answer to the question; some goes to even greater lengths to demonstrate that there is no answer, knowable or otherwise; and some (mostly recent) insists that the question itself is meaningless.

Man is made for meaning—a fact nowhere more painfully and ironically evident than in the stupendous efforts of certain late moderns to build large, meaningful personal careers precisely out of their arguments on behalf of meaninglessness!

The Bible, of course, does not attempt to argue such matters. It simply asserts that only "the fool says in his heart, 'There is no God'" (Psalm 14:1 and 53:1). An important point: the word translated from the Hebrew as "fool" actually has no precise English equivalent. It refers not to someone who is intellectually stupid but rather one who lacks the wisdom of the heart (hence "the fool says *in his heart,*" not in his head). It is not our heads lifted off our torsos and abstracting in space that let us know of God and of our desire for him, but our hearts. The Hebrew-type "fool" can assert "There is no God" because he has cut himself off from what the heart knows, and especially from what it longs for. (This cutting off he must do, if he is not to fall into despair.)

Our need for God is thus the energy that fuels all spiritual distress. But it has an important root in our fallen natures as well. For if the only God is the God spoken of in Scripture—the Holy One of Israel—then there is only one way to approach him and fulfill our desperate spiritual longing: through holiness.

Spiritual distress thus has at its core our unholiness: our tendency toward unrepented sin, our lifetime burden of sin. This key fact links spiritual distress to modern concepts of psychology yet makes clear as well the great gulf that separates purely secular psychologies from genuine healing in the Judeo-Christian mode.

The Jewish and Christian traditions claim that there is indeed a God, and that he does not take just any form but is rather—and above all else—holy and good. When Moses begged the Lord to show him His glory, God assented: "I will cause all my *goodness* to pass in front of you." Yet to be protected from the power of God's overwhelming goodness, the merely-human Moses had to enter a protected place and was able to see the Lord only, as it were, from behind (Exodus 33:19-23). So powerful is God's goodness that to see it face to face, in all its glory, is death to sinful man.

Given the reality of God's holiness, therefore, there is such a thing as objective, irreducible sin, and we human beings have the capacity to know it for what it is. As a consequence, guilt too has an objective reality. While it is true that many guilts are neurotic (in that they represent self-condemnation for merely imagined crimes), other guilts exist which cannot be analyzed or understood away: they are the response of the soul to the knowledge that it has sinned.

Secular psychology has no place for such objective guilt. All guilt, in the secular view, arises ultimately from the internalization of arbitrary social standards of the surrounding culture, usually transmitted by parents and educators. Nothing can be finally and utterly condemned, because all is "socially constructed." In the words of Fyodor Dostoyevsky's most reflective character, "Without God everything is permissible."

Guilt corrodes the personality, for it is a state we cannot endure. One way or another we will seek to rid ourselves of it. The most spontaneous way of getting rid of guilt is to use one of what Anna Freud called the "defense mechanisms"—mental gymnastics we use to hide our guilt from ourselves. We may deny that what we did is wrong, or deny that we did it at all; we may forget, or blame others, and so on.

In the interest of truth, secular psychology helps perform the salutary act of uncovering our guilt and forcing us to admit what we have done. But what then? For now we are once more burdened with guilt. Though there are exceptions, in a secular psychological analysis the approach generally taken at this point is to further "uncover" the roots of the "social (or family) constructions" that labeled our actions wrong in the first place, and then try to undo these.

In other words, in the secular view, the cure for guilt is to eliminate the standards that cause it. The adulterer who is covered with shame and remorse and cannot function because of it is restored to a sense of well-being (of sorts) by his becoming convinced that (1) his sense of guilt over sex first arose when he saw his parents in bed together and was yelled at for intruding; (2) there are other cultures where wife-swapping is routine; (3) the Ten Commandments were probably written by a bunch of "dead white European—well, Jewish, anyway—patriarchs" in around 500 B.C.; and (4) "everyone does it" anyway. Perhaps (following Ted Turner) there's some reason from time to time to consider the "Ten Suggestions," but (5) "it's ridiculous to eat yourself up because of normal, healthy urges. Lighten up!"

But if the claims of Scripture are true, then the matter is turned completely on its head. For then the entire effort to undo guilt and restore the person to a feeling of self-acceptance is itself yet another—enormously sly—self-deception: the most sophisticated of all.

Once psychotherapy proceeds past the point of uncovering what we feel guilt-ridden about and starts to explain away our guilt, it has begun a reconstruction of the very illness that made us seek help in the first place. And this drives our spiritual distress even more deeply underground. For in the Judeo-Christian view, spiritual distress over sin is not socially constructed but objectively real. It cannot be eliminated except by the means outlined in Scripture: conviction, confession, repentance, acceptance of God's forgiveness, and turning toward a holier life. If the Scriptures are true, then apart from these there is no release of guilt, no surcease of spiritual distress, and no possibility of finding genuine, lasting meaning in life.

We are made for meaning, and we will seek it out as surely as we will seek food, for "Man does not live by bread alone, but by every word that proceeds from the mouth of God." The only question is where we will look and what we will find. If we attempt to satisfy our spiritual distress without first seeking holiness, we will surely end up in spiritual prostitution: for only unclean spirits will join themselves to unclean persons. Indeed, the person burdened by unacknowledged, unconfessed, unrepented, unforgiven sin has a fatal compulsion to seek out such spirits (for reasons I will discuss in detail) in whatever guise they assume: chemical, behavioral, ideological, or religious.

Relief of Distress

Whatever the cause of our distress—in most cases it is a combination of the psychological, the biological, the symbolic, and the spiritual—our natural response is to get rid of it. But for the most part, we are not naturally inclined to turn to God for this relief. "His ways are not our ways," and we generally trust our ways to be better.

What are these ways of ours? They are, of course, legion. But they all have something in common: spontaneous manipulation, as it were, of the physiology of the brain so as to generate "pleasure" as a substitute for "pain." We may do this directly and obviously, for example by ingesting a mood-altering drug; but we may also do it more subtly and indirectly, for example by seeking out a sexual relationship for the same purpose.

But certain mechanisms with which we have been "fearfully wrought," in the words of the psalmist (Psalm 139:14), cause our pleasure-seeking methods to exact a high price. We turn now to consider these brain mechanisms. After this digression into "hard science," we will return to matters of practical living—but armed with scientific evidence for some of the great truths known to us from Scripture.

Part Three:

Fearfully and Wondrously Wrought

The Highly Complex Brain

PERHAPS THE MOST COMMON analogy used today to understand the relationship between brain and mind is that between computer hardware and its software. In both the lay and scientific literature, references abound to innate, brain-based phenomena as "hard-wired."[5] The analogy is quite useful to convey how some mental states may be related to such phenomena as a loss of neurons or a chemical insufficiency—Alzheimer's disease and some kinds of depression, for example, are "hardware" problems. Other states, in contrast, represent responses of normally functioning "hardware" to "software" events such as confusion caused by lack of information or grief in response to loss.

	Human	*Computer*
Software	*Grief*	*Poor but correct results*
	Confusion	*Corrupt input data*
Hardware	Depression	Pentium chip flaw
	Dementia	Burned out chip(s)

TABLE 1.
THE MIND:BRAIN::SOFTWARE:HARDWARE ANALOGY

But the brain, as a kind of computer, operates very differently from the desktop computers we are familiar with. Conventional computers have a fixed hardware configuration into which any number of software programs may be swapped electronically. The hardware merely implements rules that are preprogrammed into the software. In contrast, the "hardware" in biological computers—our brains—is not fixed. The "software" is simply the sum of the changes that occur over time in the hardware—that is, in the nerve cells and in the connections ("synapses") between nerve cells (and possibly, too, in complex structures within nerve cells called "microtubule assemblies"). There is actually little preprogramming; what may loosely be called "programming" occurs over time through tacit learning from experience. In brief, repetition alters the brain itself.

A good example of this kind of learning is the way that a child spontaneously learns to articulate words, starting out with crude approximations and zeroing in with ever greater precision on the correct pronunciation. The changes in the connections between neurons that mediate the learning of language have been modeled—that is, simulated—on conventional computers running special "neural network" programs. These duplicate the neurons of the brain and their interconnections. When these models are run, we can actually listen to a computer "learn" to articulate simply by repetitive experience.

The researchers at Princeton who first developed one such model started the program running at, say, 4:00 p.m. At 5:00 p.m. the computer sounded like an infant babbling; by 1:00 a.m. it sounded like a toddler;

by 8:00 a.m. it sounded like a first-grader; and by noon the next day it was speaking adult English.[6]

This description of the brain as a computer is, of course, an oversimplification. In fact the brain, from bottom to top, is more like a hierarchy of types of computers. This hierarchy parallels the stages of complexity of the nervous system in animals as we move up the various levels of the animal kingdom. Thus invertebrates, such as worms, have spinal cords and little else; simple vertebrates, such as eels, have spinal cords and brain stems; higher vertebrates, such as frogs and reptiles, have spinal cords, brain stems, and paleocortexes (somewhat more primitive cortical tissue that supports rather complex functioning, but not planning, reasoning, or language); higher vertebrates, such as dogs, human beings, and dolphins, have spinal cords, brain stems, paleocortexes, and neocortexes (cortical tissue that supports planning and, in the case of humans, reasoning and language).[7]

The neocortex is the part of the brain that we might consider as the seat of the will. Through its neurons this part of the brain mediates (this is not to say "determines") the act of selectively choosing among various options, acceding to specific impulses and resisting others. The cortex is arranged in large clusters of densely interconnected neurons. Each cell establishes connections, sometimes at great distances, to as many as a hundred thousand other cells. The lower nervous system (primarily levels 1 and 2 in figure 1, following) functions quite like an archaic, standard, one-program hardware chip, while the higher nerve cells (mostly in level 4 below, but many in level 3) function almost purely as a neural network-type computer, as just described.

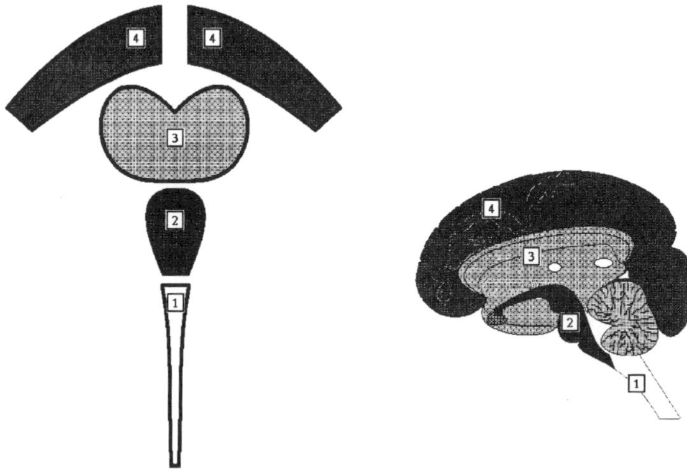

FIGURE 1: THE HIERARCHY OF BRAINS

The neocortex is also the part of the brain whose connections between neurons will be slowly modified over time, strengthening some connections, weakening others, and eliminating some entirely—all based on how experience shapes us. This ongoing process embeds the emerging pattern of our choices ever more firmly in actual tissue changes. These changes make it that much more likely for us to make the same choice with less direct effort the next time—and that much more difficult to make a different choice.

The as-yet relatively unmodified neocortex of the very young child allows him to reach out his hand to touch a hot, glowing object. No inhibitions are yet embedded in the neural network of his brain to counter the natural fascination with light and sparkle. But after sufficient experience—in this instance once may be enough—he will grow less and less likely to respond in quite the same way. There is thus a specific physical basis to learning that sheds light not only on the nature of habit, compulsion, and addiction but also on the relationship of each of these to choice.

In response to inputs to the cortex from the external world (such as touch and sight), as well as from internal stimuli (such as fear or hunger), nerve impulses travel from cell to cell over these connections. At first they travel in a random pattern, "activating" each cell at various—likewise random—levels of electrochemical excitation. The output—the thoughts and behaviors—generated by these excited cells is therefore also initially random. We easily see this kind of relatively random "output" in the rather disorganized and uncoordinated movements and sounds a newborn infant makes in response to being handled or hungry.

By contrast, behaviors that arise from lower, more primitive levels of the nervous system are quite well organized. Such behaviors include breathing, crying, swallowing, the "startle reflex" (the way an infant suddenly extends its arms and legs in response to a sudden stimulus), or the "snout reflex" (the way an infant turns its head toward an object that touches its cheek, to orient its mouth toward the nipple). These behaviors are usually the most basic and life-sustaining and are therefore also common to lower animals. By comparison to behaviors organized at the neocortical (highest) level, they are the most rigid and stereotyped, are fairly simple, and are also the least "plastic"—that is, the least subject to modification by learning and repetition.

Eventually, most of these innate behaviors become subject to selective suppression by learned, intentional behaviors mediated by the neocortex. The lower-level, innate, most primitive, preprogrammed, "hard-wired" impulses are modified by the higher, plastic, learned configurations of the brain. One example is when youngsters learn to hold their breath underwater. An infant is incapable of voluntarily suppressing the breathing mechanism in this way.

In similar fashion, some primitive mechanisms will be lost entirely: for example, when through practice a young pianist overrides the natural hardwiring that tends to make the fingers mirror one another and so learns to play parallel scales, or to break the natural tendency of the fourth and fifth fingers to move up and down together instead of separately.

When the neocortex is damaged, innate patterns re-emerge in their primitive, unmodified forms because they are truly "hard-wired." Thus we see the painfully sad reemergence of primitive responses in people with Alzheimer's disease, which slowly destroys cortical neurons to cause both a psychological "second childhood" and the re-emergence of primitive neurological reflexes such as the "startle" and "snout." The pianist who suffers head trauma may similarly find that the old "natural" patterns appear once more, and once more have to be overridden by practice.

Of course, if the neocortex is not taught properly to begin with, innate behaviors will remain in relatively primitive, unmodified form. We see this most clearly in people whose natural behaviors—especially their aggression!—should have been slowly modified over the course of many years of childhood. When this was not properly done, the adult remains "infantile." Note, too, that the proper modification involves not a total but a selective suppression of preprogrammed instinctive responses. We want to be the kind of people who do not have an apoplectic fit every time someone cuts us off in traffic; on the other hand, we want also to be able to defend ourselves effectively when genuinely in danger. (In the domain of aggression, the various martial arts, both Western and Eastern, present models of what it means thus to civilize aggression without suppressing it entirely.)

As certain connections gain in strength and others lose, which nerve cells are activated in response to stimuli, and to what degree—an enormously complex process—becomes progressively less random and more well organized. In this way learned behaviors start out quite chaotic and ineffective and become progressively more targeted, precise, and efficient. Anyone who has mastered a difficult sport or learned to play the piano has experienced this process. Indeed, we have all experienced it in most areas of life, so central is this process to human learning and action. ("By trial and error," we call it.)

It is important to emphasize that the strengthening or weakening of connections between nerve cells involves an actual increase or decrease in tissue. The strengthening of a connection requires that more and more neurotransmitter (the chemicals that signal from one neuron to another) is stored at the point of connection between nerve cells, and more and more protein receptors for these neurotransmitters are synthesized. The weakening of connections between cells likewise involves a loss of tissue. This occurs both in the diminishment of neurotransmitter and receptors and eventually in the actual dissolving of parts of the cells involved in connections that are rarely used and reinforced. This dissolving is known as "pruning." Furthermore, throughout development many new cellular connections are established for the first time. These new connections are stimulated by and come to embody physically learned behaviors. Beyond that, there is also a selective loss of neurons that are not used at all. These processes not only extend into adolescence but are especially heightened at that time, probably under the influence of dramatically altered hormones.[8]

Our Second Nature

The above section explains why it becomes ever more difficult—though not impossible—to "teach a dog new tricks" as the dog grows older. Unlike our modern computers, the brain's hardware and software are one. Therefore an old program cannot simply be swapped for a new one to be run on the same hardware. Complex patterns of behavior become progressively more deeply "embedded" in actual physical changes in the brain itself.

Incidentally, this also illustrates one of the reasons why anatomical differences in adult brains are of limited significance with respect to genetics. The differences can be acquired; they need not be innate. This point is easily missed even by presumably well-educated writers. Regarding recent research on possible brain differences in homosexuals, a reporter at the *Wall Street Journal* wrote dismissively, "Some religious fundamentalists even suggested that homosexual activity somehow could have caused the structural differences" supposedly found by a gay activist researcher.[9]

But the editor of the eminent scientific journal *Nature* commented in a response to this research, "Plainly, the neural correlates of genetically determined gender are plastic at a sufficiently early stage … Plastic structures in the hypothalamus [might] allow … the consequences of early sexual arousal to be made permanent."[10] It is worth noting that the hypothalamus is a relatively primitive, "old" part of the brain. Even such primitive parts, where most "hardwiring" is located, are subject to significant modification. The research regarding brains and homosexuality was widely—and completely inaccurately—touted by the media as evidence that homosexuality is innate.

What does "change" require and involve, then? Simply this: new patterns of behavior need to be and can be learned "on top of" the old ones. In time they will grow more and more powerful as the old ones get weaker and weaker—especially if the old ones are not repeatedly reinforced and the new ones are.

But lest we despair at the almost universal discovery that during healing our old behaviors tempt us again and again, we must remember that the old brain changes are not eliminated all at once. Furthermore, the new ones will be acquired with much greater difficulty than were the old; they are not being learned off a random, only slightly configured base, but off a base already converged into a physically, biologically shaped form.

The precise relationship in the brain among old behaviors, new behaviors and the process of change is a very specific one that is not easy to grasp (and is even more difficult to understand when we consider the effects of dramatic change, such as the change that occurs during healing prayer). To make it a bit simpler, let's turn to a diagram that is more than an analogy: it is a simplified form of the actual mathematical technique used by neuroscientists to depict brain states.

Picture, if you will, a set of possible behaviors and their associated brain "states" as a line (figure 2). A "state" is simply a list of which neurons are active at a point in time and to what degree. Each point on this line represents a different state and its accompanying behavior. The line as a whole therefore depicts, as it were, a spectrum of possible behaviors (for example, from "calm" at one end to "agitated" at the other—but the example is meant to be general, covering all possible states).

We might further imagine that this line is really a surface, like a table, viewed from one end. If it were a surface, we could map at the same time more than one dimension of our behavioral/mental/emotional states. The axis that is going "into" and "out of" the plane of the paper could now represent, say, cheerful versus angry.

FIGURE 2: A SPECTRUM FROM CALM TO AGITATED

In theory we could keep adding dimensions, one for every possible spectrum. Of course it gets increasingly difficult actually to draw such pictures as we go from one to two to three dimensions. Above three dimensions it becomes impossible. But neuroscientists can accomplish the same thing by using mathematical formulas instead and by thinking about such "higher-dimensional surfaces" by analogy to the ones we can depict in one, two, or three dimensions.

The black ball sitting on the line represents the actual mental/emotional state at present, and the fact that the line is perfectly horizontal represents the idea that the ball has no "preference" for one point on the spectrum over another (again, think of the ball as sitting on a flat table); it will not roll to any particular point (there are no "energy minima," to use technical language). The ball will, however, roll from one spot to another randomly, because the table is always "jiggling" a bit, corresponding to the fact that our brains are in ceaseless activity).

Now, this perfectly flat line (or table) can't possibly represent the mind and brain-states of an actual person, because no one has perfectly equal tendencies to every possible state. So let's change the picture in order to make it more like reality. Let's imagine that the line is like a rubber band—or better yet, that the "table" is really a sheet of rubber that can be pressed downward or upward in spots, and that will also change over time. Let's use this analogy to look at a person who has a general tendency to become agitated (figure 3; as represented by the deepest "well") and who at this moment actually *is* agitated (as represented by the fact that the ball is now in the well).

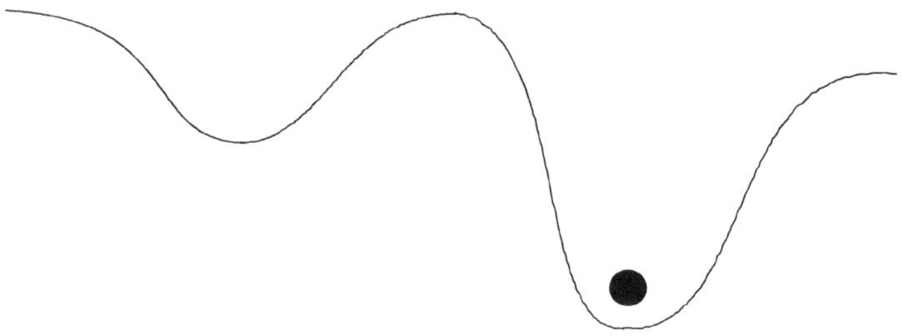

FIGURE 3:
A "WELL" REPRESENTING THE TENDENCY TO AGITATION

This person's general tendency to agitation is the end result of the complex interaction of all the factors described before—innate sensitivity, upbringing, intensity of life-stressors, a symbolic system that "reads" events as in general threatening, frequency of repetition of agitated as opposed to calm states.

We note that the ball has rolled into one of the "wells" that have been created over time (due to the constellation of current factors that interact with his disposition). We also see that there is another "well" near the calm end of the spectrum, so we understand that this person has a second tendency—coexisting with the first—to become calm. But the "calm well" is not as deep as the "agitated well." This means that all factors being equal, the individual is more likely to be agitated than calm; agitation has become "energetically more favorable" than calmness.

Now remember that the sheet is constantly jiggling (even apart from external stimuli). As a result, no state is permanently stable. Eventually a big enough jiggle will come along to jar the ball out of one well and into another (in between it will traverse a variety of other states that are only transient because they are not wells at all, but slopes or peaks). However, for this person the state of agitation is more stable than the state of calm, and it will take a bigger jolt to get him out of his agitation than it will to jar him out of his calm.

Now let's look at what happens when change occurs and new states/behaviors are learned (that is, embedded in the neural network of the brain; figure 4). The large black arrows represent various influences that are making this person generally more calm and less agitated. The part of the rubber sheet at the "calm" end is being pushed down, creating states of calm that are more "energetically favorable" (more likely, less unstable), while the part at the "agitated" end is being pushed up, making agitation less favored (less likely, more unstable).

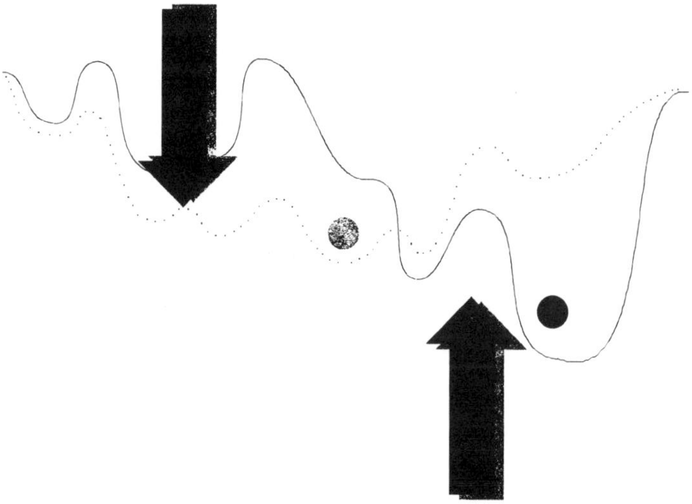

FIGURE 4: A CHANGE TOWARD GREATER CALM

But note that the original hills and valleys do not entirely disappear. They do become less and less important, however, as the process of reshaping the topography proceeds. The dotted line represents a new configuration. It shows the same basic structure as the original (that is, peaks and troughs still exist in the same locations), but its most likely (energetically favored) point has changed dramatically, shown by the faint ball in a new spot.

Behaviors become increasingly strengthened through repetition. This strengthening alters the brain physically in a way that cannot be entirely undone, if at all; it is modified with great difficulty. The more deeply embedded in the brain the old behavior has become, the greater effort of will, the more repetitions of the new behavior, and the more time will be required to modify it.

The Presence

God's presence also generates quite new patterns of behavior, sometimes abruptly. But even here, in this widely recognized but more mysterious process (the prototypical example of which is "religious conversion"), it is well known that the old patterns, and the potential for falling back into old behaviors, do not simply disappear. Can we use the model explained above to help us understand what is happening in these instances?

Neuroscientists have certainly not tried to model the quantitative effects of conversion and religious practice, since the majority have little interest in the phenomenon of faith, many are skeptical, and not a few are actively hostile. But we can put together what has long been known to objective (even if not sympathetic) observers concerning the salutary effects of faith, with what we do know of how the brain operates.

We may thus surmise the following about the effect of the presence of the Lord (see figure 5). It is as though this presence exerts a constant, persistent pull downward from a crucial point on the sheet (the place where God's Spirit touches ours would surely be the "calm" end of the calmness-agitation dimension), slowly subsuming all that we are into His "well." Thus over time it grows ever more likely that the spot to which our ball will roll is at His feet.

FIGURE 5: THE "PRESENCE"

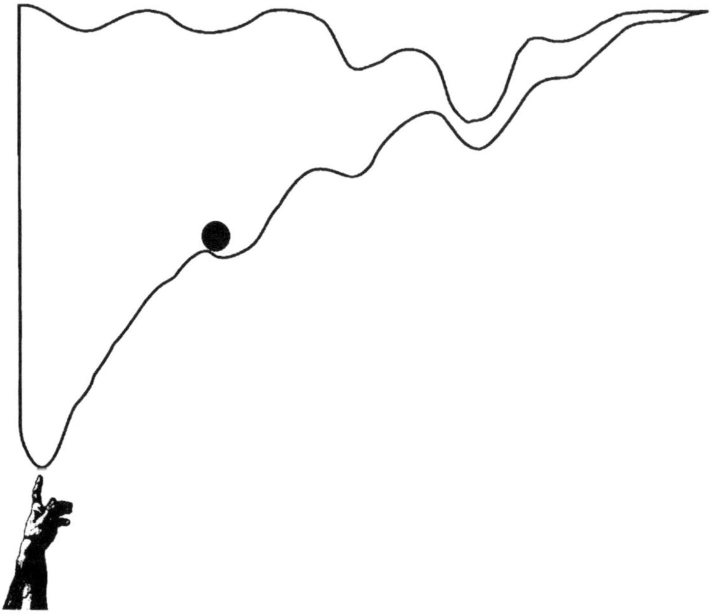

Nonetheless, note again that the old patternings have not disappeared, however much we have been drawn toward the Lord and however deep has become His imprint on our lives. (The "old man" does not disappear all at once in this lifetime, though we, in the Spirit of Messiah, are dead to him.) This lack of perfection should not be cause for despair, since the practical truth is that the longer we dwell in God, and he in us, the steeper grow the slopes that lead to his presence, and the less and less likely it is that we will be captured in the old imprints, even if they have not been erased entirely.

Pleasure Centers

Complex, multidimensional series of actions that have become habitual start out as single, individually considered, and selected choices. Later they develop into the automatic actions we call habits. Our responses, in other words, become "second nature," which is an apt term. Nonetheless, we all wish to retain final authority over these habitual responses, choosing to restrain and release them as best serves our interests, or more importantly, as is right.

The difference between a simple habit and a compulsion is partly a matter of degree. But more pertinently, *compulsions are also linked to innate, primitive impulses*. We have no natural biological urge to drive a car (although we do have a biological thrust to locomotion); we do indeed have such urges to eat, fight, and have sex.

Of all the biological drives, the sexual drive is the one linked most strongly to pleasure. Even hunger maintains its force primarily through regulatory systems in the brain that are less strongly linked to pleasure centers than is sex. However, in the "eating disorders" (as well as in certain forms of depression mediated by the neurotransmitter serotonin), eating can become so strongly linked to pleasure that the pleasure of eating overrides the discomfort of satiety.

But indeed, in light of the goal-directness of all biological systems, hunger *need* not be so strongly linked to pleasure as is sex. From a purely biological point of view, food is a genuine need of the individual, while sex is not—strange as that may sound in our society. Sex, whose biological purpose is reproduction, is rather a need of the *species.* (A person can survive without sex; a species cannot.) The pursuit of sex therefore needs to be strongly reinforced through mechanisms beyond the immediate survival of the individual.

The fearsome power of pleasure-related mechanisms in the brain is illustrated in a recent experiment with rats. They were given a lever to press that fed them a simple solution of liquid and cocaine, whose effects in the brain involve many neurotransmitter systems. The rats pressed the lever to the point of starvation, physical exhaustion, and death, ignoring hunger entirely. This controlled experiment with lower animals illustrates an outcome not so different from the life- and relationship-destroying effects of many compulsive pursuits to which human beings are prey: chemical, sexual, and otherwise.[11]

The brain has certain areas whose primary function is to create a feeling of "pleasure" only under specific circumstances. Thus, as a prime example, the pleasure areas of the brain are most intensely activated at the moment of sexual orgasm. The mechanism whereby this occurs is chemical: among the many physiological events associated with orgasm, one is the generation of a signal sent to certain nerves that travel to the pleasure areas of the brain. When the signal arrives, it causes little sealed packets at the nerve endings to open up and release their contents (neurotransmitters) onto other cells. The surfaces of these other cells have specially designed receptors that match the shape of the released chemicals in lock-and-key fashion. When the chemical binds to the receptor, the receptor sends a signal to the pleasure areas to generate the feeling "intense pleasure." (Incidentally, although we know that this mechanism triggers pleasure responses, it does not explain how we have a subjective *consciousness* of pleasure.)

In the case of pleasure, the chemical released from the nerve endings is a special type called an "opioid," meaning "opium-like." Of all behaviors, none would appear to be accompanied by so intense a burst of internal opioids as sex. Therefore, apart from the repetitive ingestion of such external opiates as heroin—the classic example of addiction—no experience is more intensely pleasurable. This fact sheds light on the ease with which repeated sexual behaviors are especially strongly reinforced.

The subjective experience of heroin addicts provides a rather startling confirmation of this chemical connection between addiction and sexuality: addicts invariably describe the pleasure of a heroin "rush" as, precisely, "orgasmic." Not surprisingly, heroin or cocaine addicts also quickly lose interest in actual sex.

The experience of pleasure creates powerful, behavior-shaping incentives. For this reason when biological impulses—especially the sexual ones—are not at least partially resisted, trained, and brought under the civilizing influence of culture and will, the pressure to seek their immediate fulfillment becomes swiftly and deeply embedded in the neural network of the brain. Furthermore, the particular, individualized patterns by which we seek this fulfillment will also become deeply implanted—even if they involve concurrent pain, as happens when childhood experiences of suffering become linked to sexuality.

Once embedded, sexual fantasy life in particular cannot simply be erased through an act of will. New fantasies may be learned "on top of," so to speak, the earlier ones; we may become highly motivated not to act on our fantasies; we may learn new behaviors that prove as gratifying as, or even more gratifying than, the old ones. The old ones will weaken and wither, yet they will always be there—the "old self" based on the "natural man" does not die entirely in this life, even though we may die (though not all at once) to self. Few are so strong that, given sufficient duress, the old patterns of fantasy and behavior could not be provoked once again into seductive strength. Recall King David, a "man after God's own heart," who nonetheless fell when sufficiently tempted. It should be emphasized, however, that these fantasies can be checked and placed, as it were, "in jail," where they can no longer reach us (and press us into reinforcing them) while we are in the process of developing a healthy imagination. There is nothing more effective in accomplishing this regeneration of our symbol system than dependence on God.

With effort and sufficient motivation, the unaided person's will may master other, non-drive-related habits. But habits linked to drive-related pleasures often overpower the will. In short order, therefore, unregulated sexual tendencies become habits, then compulsions, and finally something barely distinguishable from addictions.

Another important but subtler point made previously needs to be emphasized. The brain-based mechanisms that mediate pleasure are closely linked to those that mediate pain. Often a pleasurable experience—or at least one that arouses some aspects of our physiology to a state in which we are "hard-wired" to feel pleasure—may become linked to a painful stimulus. This occurs commonly, for example, when children are sexually abused, causing them to link sexual arousal to the "taking in" of pain. People who have suffered in this way when young often find themselves as adults confused and anguished over what seems to be an irrational compulsion to "seek out" hurtful sexual experiences and relationships. Mechanisms such as these lie behind the disproportionately high percentage of people struggling with homosexuality who were molested as children.

As has been observed by psychoanalysts, the so-called perverse forms of sexual expression (including those associated with pain) are especially likely to become compulsive: "The concept of addictive sexuality or neoneeds is ... introduced in reference to the compulsivity that invariably accompanies perverse sexuality."[12] This observation is consistent with the enormously greater promiscuity that is typical of the gay lifestyle, for example.[13] (The concept of false needs—and an understanding of their invariably compulsive nature—will be taken up in greater detail in the next section.)

These extreme variants of compulsive sexual behavior, as well as the repetitive use of pornography, prostitutes, masturbation, extramarital affairs, or even erotic fantasy, have caused considerable distress to many in our society. From a quite mundane perspective, therefore, and without an understanding of the brain processes underlying these behaviors, groups have sprung up to help people free themselves from these behaviors. Within these groups, these behaviors are wisely, if from a medical perspective somewhat imprecisely, referred to as "addictions," whose central mechanism is "dependence."

The term "dependence" might better be limited to the body's physiological response to the absence of an externally supplied chemical on which it has become reliant. In a medical context dependence on a chemical means that a normal state of physiological repose (as measured by normal vital signs—blood pressure, pulse, respiration rate, and temperature) will be disrupted, sometimes to the point of death, unless that chemical is reintroduced. (This is what a "hangover" is and why "the hair of the dog" provides temporary relief.) Dependence occurs when an external substance is regularly ingested that closely mimics the critical regulatory function of an internal chemical, as opiates mimic opioids. In time, the body is fooled by the external compound into shutting down its own natural production, until finally the person becomes dependent upon obtaining it exclusively from the outside.

But in its power or in its effects on character, the compulsive behavior caused by an addiction is actually no different from compulsive behaviors related to the way we fulfill our biological drives. As discussed above, because the reinforcement mechanism (cessation of pain, feelings of pleasure) for the biological drives is mediated by naturally occurring opioids in the brain, to call those compulsions that fall within any of the biological drives—hunger, aggression, sex—"addictions" is not far off the mark. It is especially accurate in the domain of sex. Most importantly, from a practical point of view, the methods that have proven by far the most effective in breaking true chemical addictions also prove effective in modifying compulsive behaviors.

Many people appeal to education as an element in the long-term prevention of AIDS and of other sexually transmitted diseases. Education can be effective in preventing people from ever beginning the behaviors that lead down the slippery slope to habit, then compulsion, and finally addiction. (It is much easier for the unmodified brain to learn a new lesson on a blank slate than on top of a deeply engraved counter-lesson.) But with those for whom intensely pleasurable but nonetheless risky behavior is already a habit or worse, the educational approach is notoriously ineffective. Rational ideas and recommendations carry little weight against an addict's drive for drugs or sex. Formal drug treatment programs have long abandoned exhortation and education as being useless except in supplementary roles. Addicts simply will not abandon their behaviors except under unusual and specific constraints. Likewise, arguments that homosexuals and others caught up in perverse or compulsive forms of sexual acting-out should simply "choose" a different way of life are usually equally futile.

It is this reality that creates so much confusion for well-intentioned people of God, driving them into one of two extremes: either condemning sinners for their difficulty in refraining from sin, or redefining sins out of existence.

Human Will

Let us summarize the picture we are left with of the human will in the light of science. The naive, prescientific view might picture human beings as essentially free in their choices, constrained only by obvious external physical circumstances. But the plasticity of brain structure and function confounds this simple picture. Over time, the choices we make fall into ever more predictable patterns because the pattern of choices tends to be self-reinforcing. As we practice certain behaviors, they become easier and easier, and we become "better and better" at them. As they become easier, we grow more and more likely to choose them. The more we choose them, the more deeply embedded they become, and so on. What starts out relatively free becomes ever less so as time goes on.

The lower, more general physiological mechanisms for sexual arousal are primitive, hard-wired, and very similar in animals and human beings; sexual preferences, however, linked closely both to a complex developmental process heavily influenced by the environment and to higher-level (symbolic) mental activities such as fantasizing, are subject to tremendous variability and modification, especially at the level of the cortex. Because animals have only rudimentary neocortexes—if any at all—sexual variability among animals is limited. Because humans have such extensive neocortexes, sexual variability among human beings is extraordinary, as is the profusion of ways that we may seek and find pleasure of any sort.

In order to explain why some people behave one way and others differently, the scientific approach is to examine why we begin to do certain things in the first place. In order to do that, we turn not only to our genes and hormones but to our childhoods, the influence of parents, and the influence of society. And in order to understand fully why parents act the way they do and why society acts the way it does, thereby influencing us in a predictable way, we need to keep reaching for more and more distant and more and more complex chains of causality.

Because of practical considerations, we cannot actually perform such an analysis in much detail with respect to complex behaviors. In theory, however, that is how science examines the problem: it squeezes down the tiny residual area of unaccounted-for action to a smaller and smaller point until free will can be thrown out altogether. In this view "free will" is an illusion, just a gloss for our temporary ignorance of determining causes.

Sufficiently keen observers might be able to guess how most of us might act in certain situations. In so doing, they would be suggesting that our actions are not free, but determined. And yet the reality is that we *are* free, and we hold others accountable for their actions as though they were free, too. This freedom is not provable by science[14] but is an act of faith as much for the hyperrationalist as for the fundamentalist.

Thus to the original picture of the human being as a completely free agent, science has added the discovery that though we are free, we are also nudged in this direction or that by various forces outside our control. And to those things we repeatedly choose, we become progressively bound. For this reason what starts out free may—because of those choices—turn compulsive. In the words of Rabbi Isaac cited above, "At first, sin is like an occasional visitor, then like a guest who stays for awhile, and finally like the master of the house."[15]

Part Four

False Needs

"He who makes a beast of himself gets rid of the pain of being a man."

—Samuel Johnson

Quae Gaudio Coelo

MANY YEARS AGO, my wife and I completed a beautiful library in our home, and I set up my writing desk in it. There the walls are lined with books on myriad subjects that reflect my spiritual peregrination of some not-quite-fifty years. Some books are there for reference only, but I have read most of them, some long ago. As I allow my eyes to wander over the shelves, the content of each comes briefly to mind again, along with the faint echoes of the mood it left. I am struck with the longing, the searching that drove each author. Yes, it is the same longing that is within each of us, and it is the same longing that impelled me to buy and read each of these books, however seemingly unspiritual the topic.

These books were partly responsible for teaching me a lesson—even the books that tried to assert its opposite. This lesson is that the spiritual longing of the soul has no object—no complete fulfillment—in the natural world.

In this library there also rests a stately black, gold, and red harpsichord (which I make time to play all too infrequently—alas). And the inside cover of the harpsichord is inscribed with an ancient Latin motto that expresses well both the lesson of the library and the proper relation of that library (indeed, of all material things, books and harpsichords included) to the final things: *Haec si contingant mundo quae gaudio coelo*—"If such are the pleasures of the world, what must be the joys of Heaven!"

The true object of the soul's longing is Heaven, whether we realize it or not. Though we are made of mere earthen stuff, we seem to be so constructed as to harbor desires that soar far beyond our natural limitations. We need food and drink to sustain our bodies, and so we are given hunger and thirst (and the capacity to experience satiety) to guide and constrain us in our physical "refueling." The race needs replenishment, and so we are given sex to ensure its continuance from one generation to the next. We live in a harsh, often dog-eat-dog world, and so we are given aggression to protect ourselves and our loved ones.

Each of the longings of our physical nature thus has its proper object. Hunger has food; thirst has water; sex has a beloved; and aggression has an enemy. And all of these and others not listed—all the assorted impulses and their objects—animals have, too. But how strange would we be to have been created with an additional longing for something that does not exist at all! (And it would be even stranger for us to have so *evolved,* given that evolutionary processes are widely thought as mechanical responses to mere necessity.)

The soul responds to the frustration of its in-between status—above the animals, below the angels—in many different ways. It may remain in longing but seek eagerly, perhaps even in confidence of a final success. It may sink into despair. It may attempt to flee from "the hound of heaven" and deny its longing altogether, driving it's hopes into deep hidden recesses. Or it may turn bitter and cynical toward all things of the spirit. But the universal response to this longing for Heaven—which occurs in some measure to all people at least sometimes, and to a great many as a way of life—is to *substitute* the pleasures of this world for those of the next.

Those with an intellectual cast of mind make this substitution the foundation of an entire worldview. This is what modernism is, with all its materialist ideologies. Descartes and his followers, who made a god of science; Marx and his followers, who made a god of the state; Freud and his followers, who made a god of the psyche, are preeminent among them.

Two Souls, As It Were

Traditional Judaism makes a clear distinction between the longings of the "animal soul" and the longings of a distinct and separate, higher soul that humans alone have, and that animals lack. In general usage today, this other soul is sometimes called one's "spirit." But mostly the words soul and spirit are used imprecisely and frequently substituted for one another, reflecting a loss of this ancient distinction (which was indeed once a prominent part of the Christian understanding as well).

The "animal soul" corresponds roughly to what psychoanalysts today call the "instinctive drives"—the urge to fulfill biological impulses—along with the subjective experience of those urgings. The higher soul corresponds to our need for meaning and purpose in life and to our longing for a personal relationship with an involved and loving God (this longing may take the form of simply wishing there were such a God, even if at the moment one disbelieves in him).

Animals lack this higher soul and are oriented solely toward the biological imperatives of life. Yet we may observe how an animal that has become domesticated, especially a beloved pet, seems through its capacity for love to borrow our own higher soul, and thus attaches itself to us in much the same way we attach ourselves to God.

Would it be just as clear to speak of "body and soul" as of two souls? That is certainly the conventional manner of "cutting the pie," and it has the virtue of reminding us of our physical selves and that our instinctive drives are rooted in in our bodies. And yet, there is a great value in understanding that we have two separate souls. For the true focus of what we are addressing is not something material on the one hand (the physical body itself) and something non-material on the other (the non-physical soul and its longings), but rather two non-physical sets of longings, one of which is generated by the body and the other is not.

The concurrent presence in our minds (at both conscious and unconscious levels) of both these sets of impulses and longings sets up many of the conflicts that are most distinctively human. (Conflicts between selfishness and altruism, for example.)

It helps us to keep the two sets of longings separate and disentangled, for the great error into which we are all prone to fall is to confuse the two. In fact, it is typical of the modern age to have collapsed the one entirely into the other. (The psychoanalytic claim that longing for God is merely a displaced longing for a lost childhood is an example of such a collapse, along with its conclusion that religion, therefore, is merely neurotic wish-fulfillment.) When the two are so collapsed, the upper soul, over the course of a lifetime, rather than ascending higher and higher—ever closer to the presence of the Lord—sinks downward and gets progressively dissolved, so to speak, in matter, losing all its potential glory. "The human spirit ascends on high, the spirit of the beast descends down into the earth," warns the writer of Ecclesiastes (3:21). He is speaking not merely of the differences between men and animals, but of the differences among people as well—and of the conflicting spirits within each one of us, too.

Another value in picturing ourselves as having two souls is that it reminds us that each soul has its proper set of objects and needs. Our animal natures have their proper fulfillment; our spiritual nature has likewise. Neither is to be denied.

The upper soul is often nowadays improperly taught. It is not informed by a worldview that would enable it to identify the object of its powerful longings correctly. Thus it inevitably bends downward into the created world, attempting to find fulfillment of its spiritual need (for the Creator) in the domain of the animal soul (the creature). Mankind was made to worship, as many have observed. If we do not worship God, we will not therefore cease to worship—we will worship instead the creature, which is to say just about anything. Each person will simply "select" the instinctive craving to which he is most naturally inclined (for whatever reasons, innate and acquired) and will make of it his "god."

From the Hebrew Scriptures we also learn of God's determined insistence that we avoid impure mixtures of the sacred and the profane. This is one of the inner meanings behind the puzzling, at times seemingly obsessive concern in the book of Leviticus with "ritual purity." From its distinct perspective, all "spiritual illness" consists in the impure mixture of the upper and lower souls, the sacred and the profane.

Note, too, that what is characterized in the Scriptures as profane is not necessarily evil. The rigid identification of "profane" or "earthly" with "evil" is one of the errors into which the ancient Gnostics fell, as did, unfortunately, the church itself at various times and places (in its extremes of asceticism and mortification of the flesh, for instance).

In the ancient (still current) Hebrew view, contact with a dead body, with women's menses, with non-Kosher food, with men's nocturnal seminal emissions, and with many other morally neutral objects will lead to the ritual impurity of an individual or of another sanctified object. This is not because these things are evil but because in their merely natural, fallen state they do not belong to the domain of the upper soul; they remain trapped, as it were, exclusively within the animal soul by its powerful instincts for self-preservation, reproduction, feeding, and so on. They are unsanctified, hence unredeemed.

One task of the upper soul, among others, is to lead the individual in the sanctification of the domain of the lower soul, slowly raising it upward by degree. Eating, a profane activity per se, is sanctified—made holy—by the restraints placed upon our appetites, by blessing of the Lord who created it, and by its placement at times within sacred ritual. The upper soul has no appropriate complementary task to descend and thereby to be made profane—though this, too, has formed the basis for many a Gnostic heresy (alchemy, for instance; such a false symmetry which reconciles opposites is typical of many modern "spirituality" movements as well). Neither is it possible to sanctify and redeem that which is not only profane, but evil. Evil must simply be hated:

> The Lord loves those who hate evil; he preserves the lives of his saints; he delivers them from the hand of the wicked (Psalm 97:10 RSV)

> The fear of the Lord is hatred of evil. (Proverbs 8:13 RSV)
>
> Hate evil, and love good, and establish justice in the gate (Amos 5:15 RSV)

In order for the upper soul to carry out its task of raising the individual toward God, it must first of all know that God *is*, and that he is the proper object of its distinct desires. It must be taught in many other ways as well, which is the goal of the lessons contained in Scripture.

When misdirection of the upper soul occurs, as is nowadays routine, our animal natures—our instinctive urges for food, sex, aggression, and so on—are pressed into fulfilling spiritual needs. In this effort they cannot possibly succeed. This is the process that lies at the core of compulsion and of addiction, indeed of sin and idolatry itself, the essence of "spiritual illness."

The Road to Addiction

Having previously considered the brain mechanisms whereby our experience is transmuted into our very being, we are ready for the central section of this book: a discussion of "false needs." To a "diagnostician of the soul," the presence of these needs is the symptom *par excellence* of "spiritual illness."

In her many fine books on healing prayer, Leanne Payne speaks powerfully of the "true self" and of the "false self."[16] The true self, she explains, is who we (potentially) are (and over a lifetime actually become) when we are fully in God; the false, who we turn ourselves into apart from him. No distinction could be more crucial in this frightening age, when so many are floundering in their search for identity, and so many have turned to even the basest of creaturely pursuits in a desperate attempt to solve this quintessentially spiritual problem of selfhood.

The fulfillment of our true needs (the spiritual ones included—but not exclusively) is crucial to the nurturing of our true self, and to the progressive building up and strengthening of that (and not any other) self, according to the processes just outlined. Similarly, the generating and feeding of false needs is central to the building up of a false self.

Sin and Self-Soothing

Our natural reaction to pain, as discussed above, is to rid of ourselves of it. And one of the most common methods we use is to replace pain with pleasure. But though this replacement may come to us quite naturally, it is one of the easiest roads to sin.

What is the alternative? It is what Mario Bergner calls "redemptive suffering"—that is, suffering *through* an experience in such a way that it leads to awareness of God and of our dependence on him. In his book *Setting Love in Order*, Bergner describes the many excruciating ordeals of loneliness and anxiety that he had to suffer—eschewing available routes of self-soothing—in order finally to achieve the degree of wholeness in God that led to the healing of his compulsive homosexuality.[17]

But this idea that suffering can have redemptive value—a value that even transcends personal healing—is, of course, utterly alien to the "natural man," as it is also alien to a world possessed by a naturalistic worldview. To such a world, with such a worldview, it is perfectly obvious that the only proper response to suffering is to rid oneself of it as quickly as possible. To people with the modernist outlook, the idea that to so flee from suffering might violate some "higher," non-material principle or have some adverse effect on the "soul" is the height of folly—for in this view there are no principles irreducible to material existence and no such thing as "soul" (except perhaps as a quaint metaphor for "socially constructed affective dispositions".)

And yet the idea of "redemptive suffering" lies at the very core of Christianity. Its central drama is that of the Savior whose suffering redeems. The same motif lies as well at the heart of Judaism, though this fact is little known or taught today. This is so not only in the famous suffering servant passages of Isaiah 53:

> Surely he took up our infirmities and carried
> our sorrows,
> yet we considered him stricken by God,
> smitten by him, and afflicted.

> But he was pierced for our transgressions, he
> was crushed for our iniquities;
> the punishment that brought us peace was
> upon him, and by his wounds we are
> healed.

It is evident in the understanding of the great rabbis of later centuries as well:

> Suffering and pain may be imposed on a Tzadik (righteous one) as an atonement for his entire generation. This Tzadik must then accept this suffering with love for the benefit of his generation, just as he accepts the suffering imposed upon him for his own sake .... All this involves a Tzadik who is stricken because his generation is about to be annihilated, and would be destroyed if not for his suffering ....
>
> Within this same category there is a class that is even higher than this. There is suffering that comes to a Tzadik who is even greater and more highly perfected than the ones discussed above. This suffering comes to bring about the chain of events leading to mankind's ultimate perfection ....
>
> They can therefore rectify not only their own generation, but can also correct all the spiritual damage done from the beginning, from the time of the very first sinners.[18]

Indeed, it was with this ancient knowledge in their hearts that so many Jews in the Holocaust went to their deaths with the words of Deuteronomy 6:4 on their lips: "Hear, O Israel, the Lord our God, the Lord is one." Like lambs to the slaughter, as sheep before their shearers are silent—to adapt another verse from Isaiah 53—they knew that they were dying *Kiddush Ha Shem*—"to sanctify the Name"—and that by their sacrifice others would be blessed. The Orthodox Jew of today perceives and accepts the dire, mysterious relationship between the prophetic fulfillment of Israel's re-establishment after two thousand years of exile and the Holocaust that concluded just as Israel was reborn.

Pleasure: Sacred, Profane, and Sinful

There are three ends that pleasure may serve, two of which are proper, the third not.

The *sinful* end of pleasure is as a sop for pain. In this instance the pleasurable responses of the human body—which were created deliberately by God—are being stimulated and manipulated not to fulfill the natural end for which they were designed but to hide other, often intrinsically unrelated distresses. There are many examples of this: the woman who overeats because of emotional emptiness, the promiscuous man who seeks out women to deaden his feelings of depression, the men and women who seek in homosexual unions the tenderness of genuine motherly or fatherly love they lacked as children.

The *profane* use of pleasure (remember, profane is not necessarily the same as sinful[19]) is to fulfill the natural, animal needs. These needs are genuine; they are as much a part of our physical existence as the activities that fulfill them. The fact that they are rooted in the material world does not mean they are evil: as C. S. Lewis noted, "God loves matter; he created it!" To eat when hungry, to have sex when concupiscent, to compete for reward—all these activities engaged in for the purpose of attaining natural ends are normal and not necessarily sinful. But neither, in such a state, are they sacred. Wine, per se, is neither sinful nor sacred. In Christian tradition, however, upon being blessed in the communion service it becomes a *sacra*ment, hence sacred. In Jewish tradition, upon blessing God for having created wine, it, too, is elevated and becomes holy. (The two traditions come together, of course, at the last supper, as Jesus raises the cup and repeats the traditional Jewish blessing over the wine—which is a blessing of God for creating it—and then offers it as his blood.)

One of the great confusions of the modern worldview is the resymbolizing as sacred that which is merely natural—thus creating impure mixtures of the sacred and the profane. One prominent Episcopal priest and Jungian analyst, having fallen prey to this confusion, titled one of his books *The Sacrament of Sexuality*. Marriage, which has at its heart the marital union (and hence, too, its pleasure), is sacred; but sexual pleasure per se is not. The typically modernist error of assuming that it can be leads promptly to the next: the redefining as sacred of not just the profane but evil as well.

Thus a later Jungian analyst takes the inevitable next step and tries to make sacred the consequences of sacramentalized sexual pleasure in general. Her book is therefore entitled *The Sacrament of Abortion*.

The highest end of pleasure is indeed the sacred. There is in fact no natural pleasure for which we have been designed that the Lord would deny us. But there is also no natural pleasure that God would allow us without the ordained constraints that set it apart from the merely natural in order to make it holy—to sanctify it.

Human beings are capable of an enormous diversity of sexual activities. But while it is God's intention that we should experience pleasure in sex, it is his clearly stated will that we not do so in all possible ways or settings. Indeed, many forms—really most of what is in theory possible—lie clearly "outside the boundaries." (We are here chiefly considering all the possibilities outside of faithful heterosexual marriage, not so much what is possible within.) But marital sex, which lies inside the most obvious boundary (of fidelity), can still be profane, even if not sinful. This results when it is not done in a spirit of "Kiddush Ha Shem," of sanctifying his name. All that interferes and distracts from the purity of union that God has established as the highest ideal in marriage—however large or small that interference may be—mixes the profane (and possibly the sinful, too) with the holy and so profanes it.

For example, we do not violate any of the Ten Commandments if we engage in sex within marriage simply to discharge sexual tension, but our act is then profane, and thus less than what God has designed us for.

In Judaism, sexuality is recognized as an enormously powerful force. It needs therefore to be hedged about with many constraints—even arranged marriages in some very orthodox communities. But it is also understood as a force that, when sanctified, is potentially holy to the highest possible degree. Indeed, the sanctified marital union (not sexuality in the state of nature) is poetically referred to in Judaism as the "Holy of Holies." According to Rabbi Moses Nachmanides in the thirteenth century, one of the greatest Jewish sages, there is *nothing* more holy and pure.[20]

The boundaries that are meant to limit and guide our natural impulses are not themselves natural. They come from a source outside nature and so at times cut against the grain of nature. The purpose of these boundaries is not to destroy nature but to elevate it. To be elevated it must be purified; in its natural state it is profane.

Idolatry and False Needs

Let us turn now to a closer examination of the sinful pleasures, for they are intimately connected to the preeminent sin so named in Scripture: idolatry, the worship of "gods that are no gods." To do so, it will help to consider how we satisfy our needs.

The natural (profane) order of events with respect to food, for example, is as follows: One's body uses up the store of available energy; the brain senses this via chemical and nerve-based feedback from the stomach and in the bloodstream; the brain then generates a signal to activate the nervous-system circuits responsible both for the subjective craving for food and for typical food-seeking behavior. Both the craving and the associated behavior persist until enough food is taken in to meet the brain's internal criteria, at which point both are turned off for a time.

In this rather mechanical fashion the state of hunger (subjective craving, objective behavior) is directly coupled to the genuine needs of the organism. This coupling ensures that the drive will be engaged only so long as the need is actually present and unfulfilled. The same coupling of drive to need is found with respect to all biological functions in a normal person or animal. (Of course we can't get any direct information about the subjective, craving aspect of animals' experience, we can only observe that they act as though they were experiencing craving.) We have been so designed as to be marvelously capable of fulfilling these needs under diverse conditions and in many different ways; animals are far more limited in this respect.

This capacity to respond to need includes both the simple fact that we experience needs in the first place but also that we can become consciously aware of our needs—reflecting on them introspectively—and thus able to communicate them in ways that help us fill them. Once a human child is able to speak, he can communicate his wants directly to his parents with great specificity: "I want some milk, Mommy." The family dog, however, can at best show signs of agitation to communicate in a far less precise way that he is in a state of some kind of distress.

Thus, the mental life of human beings is extraordinarily "plastic," far more so than that of animals. It is able to transform subjective inner states into symbols. (Recall our earlier discussion of the plasticity of the human brain, especially its enormous cortex, in contrast to the relative rigidity of the "animal" levels of the brain; and our discussion of "symbolic distress," our capacity to transform the meaning of stimuli according to symbolic "codes.")

But this plasticity has an unexpected result; something else that animals cannot accomplish: *Satisfying* (or "pseudo-satisfying") *a need from one domain by artificially arousing a need in another domain and satisfying it instead.* To stimulate an instinctive urge and then satisfy it for the purpose of relieving distress that has arisen in an unrelated domain is actually to create a false need.

For example: under the normal circumstances described above, we eat only when we are hungry. But it is commonplace for people to engage the hunger drive, and satisfy it, in order to meet not a physical need for food but an unfilled *emotional* need—for love or security or nurturance, or merely to stave off loneliness. And furthermore, we are so good at this that we can do it even when we are not hungry—indeed, even when we are overfull.

This, of course, is the underlying mechanism behind many of the specific "eating disorders." But such a transposition of the need for food from one domain to another is more widespread than that: this is why there are so many overweight people, whereas even in times of great plenty it is extraordinarily rare to find an overweight animal (that is, in the wild; domestic pets can acquire such human neuroses by proxy in the same way they acquire other, more noble traits).

Furthermore, false needs that have been aroused in this fashion are invariably compulsive, regardless of whether they are being used to fulfill an emotional or a spiritual hunger. There is a simple dynamic that leads directly to this compulsivity. The filling of a false need leads to a temporary experience of pleasure which, for a time, overrides the genuine need it is hiding. *But the genuine need is not being met.* After an invariably short time, then, the original distress returns, stronger than ever for having remained wholly unaddressed. The transient experience of pleasure provides but the illusion of fulfillment; the disillusionment only sharpens the true need. Immediately the craving returns, again and again, and soon a habit has been established: the habit of turning to the fulfillment of the false need whenever the true, underlying distress is aroused. And it's always aroused, because it's never filled. Undoing an established false need is hard not only because it has become deeply engraved, so to speak, but also because when it is given up, the original need returns in all its strength—and one has not ever learned how to address it properly.

To thus create a "false need"—for food, for sex, for dominance, for power, for money—is to establish a need that is neither God-given nor natural, even though it uses natural functions. (That is why the cry "But it's natural!" as an excuse for such behavior misses the point utterly.) It is, in fact, wholly unreal, and yet it comes in time to rule one's life. It is, in short, an idol exactly as described in Scripture.

For example, except in cases of true metabolic illness, genuine hunger for food never produces a food addiction. Food addictions are generated by the use of food in a futile attempt to feed other hungers. So likewise with all those activities people routinely engage in to "get rid of the pain of being a man." It is for this reason that all the unbounded forms of instinctive gratification tend, in time, to become compulsive. We see this most readily in the domain of sex. Marital sex is rarely compulsive; but all forms of sex outside of marriage—homosexuality, adultery, masturbation, sadomasochism, and other perversions—typically are.

The fact is that it is quite easy to do without "bounded" sex for extended periods of time, because bounded sex remains coupled to reality. But it is enormously difficult to do without "unbounded" sex once the habit of turning to it has been embedded in the brain. On the other hand, "bounded" sex becomes most pleasurable not by becoming perverse and therefore compulsive, but when it is truly sanctified, so that husband and wife have the profound experience of being "one flesh" in God. The laws that the Lord has established to guide and limit our appetites at once serve to press them into His service and to prevent them from becoming sinful—sacrifices on the altars of idolatry.

Part Five

Our Need for a Messiah

"And were it not that the Holy One, blessed be He, is his help, he would not be able to withstand it, as it is said, 'The Lord will not leave him in his hand, nor suffer him to be condemned when he is judged'"

—Talmud, Sukkah 52a

The Biblical View of Sin

SCIENCE CANNOT TELL US what is right and what is wrong; it can only tell us what *is* and, with respect to human behavior, elucidate for us the influences that will nudge us in this direction or that—if we let them. Understanding these forces will not tell us whether we are being nudged rightly or wrongly, although that understanding may help us go in the direction we choose.

The Bible, of course, is unapologetically ethical. It does not pretend to be scientific in the sense of explaining how things work; it mostly explains how things should be. It begins with the startling premise that the entire world is not as it should be: nature itself is broken, right from the beginning. Nature itself has become, if you will, unnatural—human nature included.

In today's secular culture, the biblical word sin is simply understood to refer to actions that are in some sense "wrong." It carries the musty overtones of a moralism that is both quaint and cruel. But the full biblical description of sin is far more radical and illuminating than this. The Bible describes most sins as pleasurable, natural, and self-reinforcing to the point of compulsion. They are, in effect, the addictions.

This view of sin contrasts sharply with individualistic modern morality which more or less asserts that nothing is sinful that does not immediately harm someone else. The Bible certainly agrees that harm to others is evil, but it also offers a distinctive definition of self-harm that derives directly from the first and greatest commandment: "Thou shalt have no other gods before me."

Addiction specialists emphasize how any addiction slowly, insidiously, and relentlessly removes addicts from real relationships with other people, reorienting them exclusively to the objects of their addictions. The Bible views the same process as characteristic of sin, but with an important added dimension: sinners are progressively removed not only from relationships with other people as they increasingly focus on the sin and the pleasure it affords, but also from a relationship with God.

The Bible thus sees a vital dimension to sin: it is not only increasingly addictive but a form of idolatry. The object of the sinful compulsion slowly erodes and replaces all other desires, eventually even displacing God himself, the one who should be the object of our deepest yearning. In this way we literally worship and fall into the grip of a part of creation instead of the Creator. Thus the primary criticism of human nature found in the Bible is that, for example, of the apostle Paul, describing all fallen men in their violation of the first commandment: "who changed the truth of God into a lie, and worshipped and served the creature more than the Creator" (Romans 1:25 KJV).

What is true of individuals, the Bible claims, is equally true of whole civilizations. Thus in its repeated—compulsive—falls into the snare of idolatry, the spiritual history of Israel tells much the same story as that of all nations. And the idolatry warned against in both Hebrew and Christian Scripture is not some vague intellectual nodding to a wood or stone model, but rather the repeated attraction to an ecstatic, pagan, orgiastic form of nature-worship involving both male and female ritual prostitution in an unlimited variety of sexual forms. The overwhelming power of sexual gratification is what makes it so susceptible to becoming a true compulsion. The Bible therefore most often condemns ritualized sexual compulsion as a quintessential act of idolatry. God's great patience in deferring judgment on Israel reflects his understanding that sin is more like an addiction than a simple choice: people cannot conquer it through mere moral suasion.

In Old Testament times in the Near East this idolatry took the form of the worship of Baal and Ashtoreth; in New Testament times in the Mediterranean basin it became the worship of other female deities, such as Diana at Ephesus or Aphrodite at Corinth.[21] A biblically informed perspective on our own era would consider it to be similarly idolatrous: dominated by materialistic erotic hedonism undergirded by a secularized, skeptical, or pop-spiritual, quasi-occult theology.

In the Christian continuation of the Hebrew Bible's presentation of sin, a unique and specific role is outlined for a Savior: his atoning sacrifice is capable of effecting not only forgiveness but genuine liberation from the compulsive grip of sin. This story makes even more explicit sin's power and the impossibility of mere willful change, first described in the eighth century B.C. by the prophet Jeremiah:

> Can the Ethiopian change his skin or the
> leopard its spots?
> Neither can you do good who are accustomed
> to doing evil. (13:23)

I but Not I

Many passages and stories in both the Old and New Testaments illustrate how sin is self-reinforcing, leading to an ever deeper entanglement. It is often referred to as a "snare," suggesting that as with all habits that develop into compulsions, sinful pleasures present themselves first as options, only later revealing their true power over the will. Sinners deny the potential for entrapment, inadvertently ensuring that the snare will pull tight about them before they know they are trapped. As quoted earlier, sin itself prevents resistance to it:

> The evil deeds of a wicked man ensnare him;
> the cords of his sin hold him fast.

> He will die for lack of discipline, led astray by
> his own great folly (Proverbs 5:22-23).

And St. Peter notes, "A man is a slave to whatever has mastered him" (2 Peter 2:19).

We know from the modern psychology of compulsions that when we are "mastered" by false needs, "denial" takes over as a specific mechanism, subverting any residual suspicion that escape is even desirable. What is actually a frightening vice (and a vise) disguises itself as virtue. Jeremiah describes this state of blindness in a famous passage: "The heart is deceitful above all things, and desperately wicked [or 'beyond cure']: who can know it?" (17:9 KJV).

If and when we awaken fully to our true state, it is usually far later than we had realized, for our psyche has already become configured by our behavior, a blueprint has been "burned into" the synaptic connections of the brain:

> Judah's sin is engraved with an iron tool, inscribed with a flint point,
> on the tablets of their hearts ... (Jeremiah 17:1)

Those sinners who at last awaken to the truth—like addicts who have broken through their denial—describe their state with brutal realism. For nearly two thousand years Paul's anguished description of the conflict between the two souls and of human bondage to appetite has remained among the most eloquent ever penned:

> I do not understand what I do. For what I want to do I do not do, but what I hate I do .... For I have the desire to do what is good, but I cannot carry it out. For what I do is not the good I want to do; no, the evil I do not want to do—this I keep on doing .... In my inner being, I delight in God's law; but I see another law at work in the members of my body, waging war against the law of my mind and making me a prisoner of the law of sin at work within my members ....What a wretched man I am! Who will rescue me from this body of death? (Romans 7:15-24)

Paul, himself a Talmudic pupil of Rabbi Gamaliel, answers his own query: he will be rescued only by "Jesus Christ our Lord." Thus he echoes in Christian form the Talmud's similar response to the intractable problem of the Evil Inclination, in a continuation of the passage quoted above: "And were it not that the Holy One, blessed be He, is his help, he would not be able to withstand it, as it is said, 'The Lord will not leave him in his hand, nor suffer him to be condemned when he is judged'" (Sukkah 52a).

Keep in mind our own street phrase "a monkey on my back," which refers to addiction. In the context of a discussion of sin, compulsion, and addiction, Paul's figure of speech—"this body of death—"is especially apt. It refers to the way a death sentence was often carried out in Imperial Rome. A dead body was strapped to the back of the condemned man so that he could not free himself, however he struggled. In time the putrefaction of the corpse spread and ate away his own tissues as well, slowly killing him.

All Too Natural

It is a commonplace to think of certain sins as "unnatural." As we all know, one of the most frequent barbs hurled at homosexuals and other people who practice sexual behavior other than heterosexual intercourse is that their practices are "unnatural." Paul's letter to the Romans makes a similar accusation:

> Because of this [worshiping and serving created things rather than the Creator], God gave them over to shameful lusts. Even their women exchanged natural relations for unnatural ones. In the same way the men also abandoned natural relations with women and were inflamed with lust for one another. Men committed indecent acts with other men, and received in themselves the due penalty for their perversion. (Romans 1:26-27)

But Paul's use of unnatural here is only half the story. As implied in his references to "my sinful nature" and to "another law at work in the members of my body," the more basic issue in assessing the concept of sin from a scientific and biological perspective is the fact that all forms of sin are natural. Sin is even theologically natural in a fallen world. It is unnatural only in contrast to the nature of the world as it was intended to be—the ideal world our souls have all but forgotten, whose perfection our minds but dimly perceive, our hearts desperately long for, and our actions only rarely foreshadow.

The term sin points toward a standard outside of nature (and thus outside the domain of science). Stealing, after all, is merely the natural extension of hoarding (widespread in animals, which naturally steal each other's food whenever they can); murder is the natural extension of self-protection and dominance; adultery is the natural expression of the biological drive to propagate one's own DNA as widely as possible in preference to others ("It's in Our Genes!" trumpeted a recent meaningless headline—about adultery—in a major newsweekly), and so on.

Paul's use of the term natural in the passage above has a different meaning, one he takes for granted: that the "natural use" of sexuality is primarily for reproduction, and that the sexual organs are physically designed for one specific type of sexual use.

But the Bible is filled with many references that point not to the unnaturalness of sin (including homosexuality, among many others) but to its naturalness. The Pentateuch's 613 commandments, the requirement of daily animal sacrifice for atonement, the terrible punishments meted out against certain sins—all these point to the ubiquity and deep-rootedness in human nature of what God calls sin.

The revelation at Sinai in particular, but earlier covenants as well, illustrates that God's ongoing involvement in the life of humanity represents a disruption of the fallen natural order. Sin is defined by God, not by nature. Sin is therefore not against nature but against God:

> Against you, you only, have I sinned and
> done what is evil in your sight,
> so that you are proved right when you speak
> and justified when you judge (Psalm 51:4).

So natural is sin, and so unnatural are God's requirements, that almost the entirety of the Bible tells the story of mankind's inability to obey these requirements through its own natural effort. The Bible shows the desperate human need for supernatural assistance in even approximating a godly existence:

> There is not a righteous man on earth
> who does what is right and never sins.
> (Ecclesiastes 7:20)
> Surely I was sinful at birth,
> sinful from the time my mother conceived
> me. (Psalm 51:5)

We, like the ancient Jews, therefore anticipate that the conquering of sin ultimately requires someone whose origins and nature are not entirely natural, and a process that violates the natural order of things:

> Therefore the Lord himself shall give you a sign; Behold, a virgin shall conceive, and bear a son, and shall call his name Immanuel. Butter and honey shall he eat, that he may know to refuse the evil, and choose the good. (Isaiah 7:14-15 KJV)

Even in Judaism, in which the promised redeemer is human, albeit extraordinary, tradition holds that he has existed with God since the creation:

> "And God saw the light that it was good." This is the light of Messiah ... to teach you that God saw the generation of Messiah and His works before He created the universe, and He hid the Messiah ... under His Throne of Glory. Satan asked God, Master of the Universe: "For whom is this Light under your Throne of Glory?" God answered him, "It is for the Messiah who is to turn you backward and who will put you to scorn with shamefacedness."[22]

And furthermore, it is the suffering of the righteous—not just of the sinners—that keeps the world from destruction. In the Christian faith, redemption is understood as possible only because of supernatural intervention:

> But while he thought on these things, behold, the angel of the Lord appeared unto him in a dream, saying, Joseph, thou son of David, fear not to take unto thee Mary thy wife: for that which is conceived in her is of the Holy Ghost. And she shall bring forth a son, and thou shalt call his name Jesus: for he shall save his people from their sins.

> Now all this was done, that it might be fulfilled which was spoken of the Lord by the prophet, saying,
>
> "Behold, a virgin shall be with child, and shall bring forth a son, and they shall call his name Emmanuel," which being interpreted is, God with us. (Matthew 1:20-23 KJV)

Because God knows how unnatural it is for us not to sin, he refrains from swift, talonic judgment and tempers his response with patience and mercy:

> … He does not treat us as our sins deserve or
> repay us according to our iniquities.
> For as high as the heavens are above the
> earth, so great is his love for those who
> fear him ….
> As a father has compassion on his children, so
> the LORD has compassion on those who
> fear him;
> for he knows how we are formed, he remembers that we are dust. (Psalm 103:10-11, 13-14)

The problem lies in the fact that after the Fall nature itself—including human nature—is sinful: "God saw how corrupt the earth had become, for all the people on earth had corrupted their ways" (Genesis 6:12).

The Suffering One

In the biblical view, God sent his Word—the Torah—into the corrupted natural world. From this perspective the entire question of right and wrong cannot be addressed without an understanding of and dependence on this Word. Absent this, with a viewpoint that sees only nature, "right" and "natural"—the sacred and the profane—will soon collapse into one another. We resist the sin that is natural to us only with the greatest of effort. We require the guidance of this Word in order to achieve even limited success:

> I have hidden your word in my heart that I might not sin against you.
> Praise be to you, O LORD; teach me your decrees.
> With my lips I recount all the laws that come from your mouth.
> I rejoice in following your statutes as one rejoices in great riches.
> I meditate on your precepts and consider your ways.
> I delight in your decrees; I will not neglect your word.
> Do good to your servant, and I will live; I will obey your word. (Psalm 119:11-17)

But even this was not enough; the Israelites repeatedly lapsed back into the orgiastic worship of idols and the ritual killing of the offspring that followed. Eventually, in the Christian continuation of this great drama, in order to save his children from the overwhelming power of what their own natures had become through the Fall, God made this supernatural Word literally flesh (John 1:14). He thereby began the process of transforming the flesh into his Word.

The Redeemer's life thus is the story of a Righteous One who completely refrains from that which is merely natural to do that which is right. Not only did he thereby lose his own life, but he appeased the anger of a just God at all humanity's sins—an anger that was poured out on him during his death. In mercy God withheld his wrath from his all-too-human children: "For God so loved the world that he gave his one and only Son, that whoever believes in him shall not perish but have eternal life" (John 3:16).

The natural desires of the flesh are not only nor even primarily sexual desires but all the selfish cravings to which we are natively inclined. The power to overcome them finally cannot and does not arise from nature, nor from within ourselves as a matter of simple choice, nor from complex technique. But rather, "to all who received him, to those who believed in his name, he gave the right to become children of God—children born not of natural descent, nor of human decision or a husband's will, but born of God" (John 1:12-13). Because "flesh gives birth to flesh, but the Spirit gives birth to spirit" (John 3:6).

In fact, the very ability to know the saving truth, to be convinced that God's Word is what he says it is, also does not arise from nature nor solely from human will, but is itself a gift from God:

> "But what about you?" he asked. "Who do you say I am?"
>
> Simon Peter answered, "You are the Christ, the Son of the living God."
>
> Jesus replied, "Blessed are you, Simon son of Jonah, for this was not revealed to you by man, but by my Father in heaven." (Matthew 16:15-17)

The Battle between the Lower and Upper Souls

Sin is so natural to us, and we are so utterly helpless, so unable to resist it by our own power, that we inevitably either deny that we sin or must depend upon God even to know what we need to know to begin to resist it. If God chooses not to help us, we are lost:

> He told them [the apostles], "The secret of the kingdom of God has been given to you. But to those on the outside everything is said in parables so that,
>
> 'they may be ever seeing but never perceiving,
> and ever hearing but never understanding;
> otherwise they might turn and be forgiven!'" (Mark 4:11-12)

Indeed, to be given over to our own wishes, bereft of restraint or guidance, is itself God's punishment: in the end, he gives us precisley what we clamor for. It is thus *because* people exchanged God for idols of their own devising that

> God gave them over in the sinful desires of their hearts to sexual impurity for the degrading of their bodies with one another .... Since they did not think it worthwhile to retain the knowledge of God, he gave them over to a depraved mind, to do what ought not to be done. They have become filled with every kind of wickedness, evil, greed and depravity. (Romans 1:24, 28-32)

This "depraved mind" is deeply rooted in nature itself (it is "our" nature) and thus has a sinful disposition which finally is unconquerable by natural means: "the sinful mind[23] is hostile to God. It does not submit to God's law, nor can it do so" (Romans 8:7).

Understanding the molecular mechanisms that undergird the impulses of the flesh will not illuminate the standards of the Spirit. Nor will it release us to operate in accord with those standards:

> Are ye so foolish? having begun in the Spirit, are ye now made perfect by the flesh? (Galatians 3:3 KJV)

> For the flesh lusteth against the Spirit, and the Spirit against the flesh: and these are contrary

> the one to the other: so that ye cannot do the things that ye would. (Galatians 5:17 KJV)

In other words, the natural is sufficient neither to point us toward what is right in God's eyes nor to carry us there. This is not to deny the evidence for divine will both in nature and in human nature, but knowledge of the laws of nature is not enough for us to live a godly life, merely a natural one.

And, more to the point, the fact that our nature drives us toward certain activities does not mean that these activities must therefore not be sinful. In Jesus' words:

> If your hand causes you to sin, cut it off. It is better for you to enter life maimed than with two hands to go into hell, where the fire never goes out. And if your foot causes you to sin, cut it off. It is better for you to enter life crippled than to have two feet and be thrown into hell. And if your eye causes you to sin, pluck it out. It is better for you to enter the kingdom of God with one eye than to have two eyes and be thrown into hell. (Mark 9:43-47)

Moral Standards Are Unnatural

The morality that God demands of man stands in contrast to the standards of behavior that come to him naturally. Precisely because these standards go against our nature, we need be reminded of God's law every day of our individual lives; as must every generation recall this law and claim it anew for itself. Thus the ancient Israelites were commanded at Sinai always to wear specially woven *tzitzit* or "tassels." (Observant Jewish men wear them to this day under their street clothes on a special four-cornered garment; you may observe the *tzitzit* themselves hanging down at the waist; they are the "fringe of his garment" through which in the Gospel accounts Jesus heals a woman ill for twelve years. [Matthew 9:20-22][24]) The Lord tells Moses why:

> Speak to the Israelites and say to them: "Throughout the generations to come you are to make tassels on the corners of your garments, with a blue cord on each tassel. You will have these tassels to look at and so you will remember all the commands of the LORD, that you may obey them and not prostitute yourself by going after the desires of your own heart and eyes." (Numbers 15:37-39)

The natural self, far from being worshiped because of being natural, is to anticipate suffering: "For we know that our old self was crucified with him so that the body of sin [see above, "the body of this death"] might be done away with, that we should no longer be slaves to sin" (Romans 6:6).

Modern man reflexively revolts against the assertion that God's morality stands in opposition to his natural self, and gladly abandons such conceptions as archaic. But ancient people did likewise, as Paul observed around him: "But the natural man receiveth not the things of the Spirit of God: for they are foolishness unto him: neither can he know them, because they are spiritually discerned" (1 Corinthians 2:14 KJV).

The modern mind sees the demand that we live to some extent against our own natures as merely foolish, or misinterprets it as implying a radical asceticism that would reject all forms of pleasure. But it sees as truly cruel the judgment that supposedly falls on us for not being willing to resist our genetic influences. To the modern mind, as to ancient pagans, our bodies are ours to do with as we please so long as we feel we harm no one else. But such seemingly evident notions are not the biblical view at all:

> Do you not know that your body is a temple of the Holy Spirit, who is in you, whom you have received from God? You are not your own; you were bought at a price. Therefore honor God with your body (1 Corinthians 6:19-20).

Of those who deny God altogether, in order to do as they wish, the psalmist cries out:

> The fool[25] says in his heart, "There is no
> God."

And they are fools because of what their denial leads to:

> They are corrupt, their deeds are vile; there is
> no one who does good. (14:1)

Free, Yet Slaves

Circumcision is the preeminent, unnatural mark of the agreement between Israel as carrier of God's standard and God himself. By its very nature—the removal of a natural, universally occurring piece of the male organ—it points to the unnaturalness of his law, showing how the law stands as a modification of, and even in opposition to, the purely natural impulses (perhaps especially so with regard to the sexual impulses): "You are to undergo circumcision, and it will be the sign of the covenant between me and you" (Genesis 17:11).

With the establishment of this covenant—a covenant that is some precise measure contrary to nature—humanity is put on notice of just what God's standards are: "I had not known sin, but by the law: for I had not known lust, except the law had said, Thou shalt not covet" (Romans 7:7 KJV).

And yet the mere fact of this standard does not yield compliance with it. Thus the unfolding history of Israel over the fifteen hundred years following the establishment of the covenant is one of almost unremitting failure. In the Christian understanding, divine intercession alone can reverse this failure:

> For what the law was powerless to do in that it was weakened by the sinful nature [KJV: "the flesh"], God did by sending his own Son in the likeness of sinful man [KJV: "of sinful

> flesh"] to be a sin offering. And so he condemned sin in sinful man. (Romans 8:3)

From a certain perspective it might seem strange that God would establish a standard of behavior impossible for us to meet. This is the perspective of those who claim that the naturalness of an impulse contradicts its potential sinfulness. But from the Judeo-Christian point of view, when we honestly confront what our natures, left to their own devices, really are—and what in the way of suffering they produce—we can only be grateful that we have been granted a vision of genuine goodness, however far beyond our grasp. In this state of sorrow at our inadequacy, we can turn from prideful dependence on ourselves to voluntary dependence on God. But of course, against this surrender our pride has always urged us, and urges us still, to rebel.

And indeed, from the very beginning, it is as we consider what is good and what is evil in the light of our natural cravings that our pride insinuates its own, independent, and natural standards:

> "You will not surely die," the serpent said to the woman. "For God knows that when you eat of it [the tree of knowledge] your eyes will be opened, and you will be like God, knowing [determining for yourself what is] good and evil." (Genesis 3:4-5)

The chief result of the Fall is that we now determine for ourselves what is right and what is wrong.

But in this self-determination we are far less free and independent than the serpent's lie convinces us we are. In fact, to our natural, impulse-driven compulsions we are slaves and do not know it, comfortable in a state of bewitchment. In modern language, we are in denial.

Into this cold, Luciferian illusion of freedom from sin, freedom from the consequences of choice, and darkness masquerading as illumination, God shone on ancient Israel the true searchlight of a law above, outside of and prior to fallen nature.

But except insofar as God, knowing our fallen nature, had already planned how the intrusion of his law would unfold in history, this law has not accomplished what it seemed intended to. Rather than bringing about a transformation of character from the natural to the spiritual, it accomplished just the reverse, stimulating, it seems, an even worse rebellion. Thus, foretelling the destruction of Judah and the forced exile of the people by the Babylonians, God states through Jeremiah:

> But I gave them this command: Obey me, and I will be your God and you will be my people. Walk in all the ways I command you, that it may go well with you. But they did not listen or pay attention; instead, they followed the stubborn inclinations of their evil hearts. They went backward and not forward. From the time your forefathers left Egypt until now, day after day, again and again I sent you my

> servants the prophets. But they did not listen to me or pay attention. They were stiff-necked and did more evil than their forefathers. When you tell them all this, they will not listen to you; when you call to them, they will not answer. Therefore say to them, "This is the nation that has not obeyed the LORD its God or responded to correction. Truth has perished; it has vanished from their lips." (7:23-28)

The light of God's law not only has made the darkness of human nature stand forth for what it truly is, but by contrast seems to darken it further. As Paul put it:

> But sin, seizing the opportunity afforded by the commandment, produced in me every kind of covetous desire .... Did that which is good, then, become death to me? By no means! But in order that sin might be recognized as sin, it produced death in me through what was good, so that through the commandment sin might become utterly sinful. (Romans 7:8-13)

Biblical history reveals that the attempt to establish by prescription alone a moral standard outside of nature is all too often futile—even when the prescription comes from God. Within a few generations at most, the habit of obedience to such a prescribed standard degenerates into little more than hypocritical conventions that hide the greatest degree of instinctive gratification possible. This statement about a people's relation to the Heavenly tribunal may with equal accuracy be made of the individual sinner in relation to institutional tribunals of judgment: "the attempt to force a person, by prescription alone, to adhere to a moral standard outside of nature is often futile. His obedience to such a prescribed standard is usually temporary and soon degenerates into convention and hypocrisy." This is the essence of compulsion. The God who prescribes those moral standards, who is our Creator, King and Judge, must be our Redeemer as well. If not, argues the Bible, we are lost.

The Modern Basis for Morality

As it was in ancient Israel, so it is in the modern world. Today the most widely accepted philosophy of morals, which is more commonly implicit than explicit, comes from psychoanalysis as rooted in Freud. This view holds that conscience and guilt are culturally relative and derive from nothing more substantial or absolute than learned restrictions. Because these restrictions oppose the natural impulses, they engender needless emotional conflict between genuine natural (read: "healthy") desires and artificial, unnatural (read: "unhealthy") goodness.

Sometimes these emotional conflicts are accepted as a necessary price for social orderliness; increasingly often, as the quest for pleasure and immediate gratification spreads widely, they are held to be unnecessary. In this view, these internal conflicts are passed on from one generation to the next, foolishly and uselessly, with no absolute basis whatever in either biology or spirit,[26] until enlightened would-be liberators arise to free us from them. "Overpopulation has made [the Levitical injunction against homosexuality] as irrelevant as refrigeration has made the injunction against eating pork," one pastor asserts.[27]

Although many people claim to hold to a Judeo-Christian philosophy, the psychoanalytic point of view has deeply reinforced a widespread, modern version of pre-Christian, pre-Judaic, pagan morals in our society. Some people—many leaders of churches and synagogues included—recognize modern moral standards as pagan and advocate them as such, considering the replacement of God's law by paganism as not at all going "backward," but "forward."

Modern man thus deals with the problem of guilt in two inconsistent ways. On the one hand he loosens most restrictions as archaic, arbitrary, and unnecessary; on the other hand, through social pressure and legal sanction he reinforces only those restrictions that the shifting tide of fashion—both lay and expert—deems minimally necessary to sustain order. If morality, and therefore also conscience, has no absolute basis, then there is no just cause to restrict the private or, when more than one person is involved, mutually agreed-upon gratification of impulse.

But this wholesale casting off of moral restraint and therefore of the reality of a gracious, forgiving God has the inevitable, if on the surface somewhat surprising, psychological consequence of only increasing deep-seated feelings of condemnation and guilt. This occurs for the simple reason that human beings do indeed have a conscience that is not reducible to merely natural functions. It is genuine, and it reflects in some measure, if imperfectly, the divine standard that is its source and prototype.

When we transgress this conscience (as we are increasingly apt to do absent belief in its transcendent source and reality), we suffer its pangs. To escape these pangs, we drive ourselves with increasing mercilessness to further deny its reality in the vain hope that we may thereby escape it. Like Euripides pursued by the Furies, the harder we run, the deeper into our souls are sunk the pursuing talons. And yet we will suffer almost anything, even death it seems, to avoid accepting the yoke of Heaven. With the loss of a deeply held belief in a just God and in his saving grace, God's standards not only become meaningless but actually tend to reinforce sin. The rebellious spirit is nowhere more powerfully stimulated than in the presence of authority, especially authority perceived as both arbitrary and vulnerable.

The consequences of the modern view of morality lie all about us in the disordering of relations between men and women and in the resulting destruction of the family. The fierce campaign still being waged to normalize unconstrained human impulse represents not merely the weakened moral authority of church and synagogue, but more importantly a widespread loss of faith in a just but gracious and truly transcendent God. This is true however loudly it may be denied by those who claim as a sanctified way of life any form of mere hedonistic individualism:

> But, dear friends, remember what the apostles of our Lord Jesus Christ foretold. They said to you, "In the last times, there will be scoffers who will follow their own ungodly desires." These are the men who divide you, who follow mere natural instincts and do not have the Spirit. (Jude 17-19)

Psychologically, the keenest solution to the problem of guilt—and to the problem of how the guilt and condemnation of self or others drives us ever more deeply into doing the very things that make us guilty—does not lie in the biological, social, or psychoanalytic direction of "analyzing." We cannot eliminate guilt by merely seeing through it to its supposed origins, convinced that we have thereby dissolved it into nothingness. That way leads inevitably to personal and social decay. Rather, the solution lies in maintaining conviction of our sin and yet, in a seeming paradox, understanding that God can and will lift that judgment. Paul describes this state as follows:

> I care very little if I am judged by you or by any human court; indeed, I do not even judge myself. My conscience is clear, but that does not make me innocent. It is the Lord who judges me. (1 Corinthians 4:3-4)

Notes

[1] *Midrash Rabbah* on Genesis 22:6, in *The Soncino Midrash Rabbah* (Brooklyn: Judaica Press, 1983). CD-ROM version © Davka Corporation and the Institute for Computers in Jewish Life (Chicago, 1992-1995).

[2] For a particularly powerful story of such healing, see Mario Bergner's *Setting Love in Order* (Grand Rapids, Mich.: Baker book House, 1995).

[3] R. Lau et al., "Trends in Sexual Behavior in a Cohort of Homosexual Men: A Seven-Year Prospective Study," *International Journal for the Study of AIDS* 3, no. 4 (1992): 267-72; A. Lifson, "Men Who Have Sex with Men: Continued Challenges for Preventing HIV Infection and AIDS [Editorial]," *American Journal of Public Health* 82, no. 2 (1992): 166-67; S. Adib et al., "Prediction of Relapse in Sexual Practices Among Homosexual Men," *AIDS Education and Prevention* 3, no. 4 (1991): 293-304; "Patterns of Sexual Behavior Change Among Homosexual/Bisexual Men: Selective U.S. Sites, 1987-1990," *Morbidity and Mortality Weekly Reports* 40, no. 46 (1991): 792-94; L. S. Doll et al., "Homosexual Men Who Engage in High-Risk Sexual Behavior: A Multicenter Comparison," *Journal of Sexually Transmitted Diseases* 18, no. 3 (1991): 170-75; C. Kuiken et al., "Risk Factors and Changes in Sexual Behavior in Male Homosexuals Who Seroconverted for Human Immunodeficiency Virus Antibodies," *American Journal of Epidemiology* 132, no. 3 (1990): 523-30.

[4] In an article posted to the sci.med.aids newsgroup on the Internet (message id 24405@sci.med.aids, 14 Jun 1995), Udo Schüklenk, a researcher at the Centre for Human Bioethics at Monash University in Australia, argues (to a newsgroup

subscribed to largely by homosexual men who have AIDS or are HIV positive as well as people involved either directly in their care or in the "politics of AIDS" and AIDS funding):

> A number of authors have pointed out that gay men might have rational (i.e., acceptable) reasons for having risky sex. [E.g., J Sex Res 1992 29(4):561-568; J Sex Res 1993 30(4):344-346; Bioethics 1987 1(1):35-50; Health Care Analysis 1994 2(3):253-261]...different value judgments of health promoters and sexually active individuals about the value of unsafe sex vs. the value of a long life have led to different conclusions as to what is acceptable individual behavior....Obviously to many gay men (perhaps the majority)...safe sex and fun seems to be a contradictio in adjecto [contradiction in terms]...Public health campaigns assume that health is of a paramount value and that all other individual values must have a lower ranking. Hence they do not accept that certain types of sexual risk behavior can be the best of the available solutions...I suggest that indeed certain types of motives for unsafe sexual behavior are rational and acceptable forms of autonomous decision making processes that should be accepted just as liberal societies accept other kinds of risk-taking for the sake of pleasure maximization.

A similar argument was published in *the Medical Journal of Australia* 157:846 (1992).

[5] See, for example, J. Maddox, "Is Homosexuality Hardwired?" *Nature* 353 (September 1991): 13.

[6] C. Sejnowski and C. Rosenberg, "NetTalk: A Parallel Network that Learns to Read Aloud," in *Neurocomputing: Foun-*

dations of Research, ed. J. A. Anderson and E. Rosenfeld (Cambridge, Mass.: MIT Press, 1988).

[7] This section may well start the reader wondering about evolution, and indeed, the sequence of complexity just outlined parallels the idea of "age" in evolutionary theory, with the least adaptable, most mechanical and simplest levels of the brain being the oldest. Readers with scientific expertise may be interested in a recent article published in *Science* which casts significant doubt on classical theories of evolution. Researchers discovered that as new levels of brain are added—providing wholly new functions for an organism—each older level also increases in complexity within its own unrelated domain of function in a perfectly orchestrated fashion.

The theory of natural selection holds that a new function (and the brain structure responsible for it) arises out of a plethora of mutations, each of which (if not fatal) performs a different function in the individual bearing it. Competition allows the one with the most adaptive new mutation to survive and reproduce in preference to the others, thus resulting in a new species characterized by this additional function.

However, this model cannot account for simultaneous coordinated advances in all brain functions and in each of their associated structures found by the researchers. The degree of coordination strongly suggests, rather, an orderly overarching blueprint. B. Finlay and R. Darlington, "Linked Regularities in the Development and Evolution of Mammalian Brains," *Science* 268 (June 1995): 1578-84.

[8] This process is most dramatically illustrated in schizophrenia. Once thought to be a purely psychological condition caused by inadequate mothers, it is now understood to be a developmental abnormality of the brain that occurs during intrauterine life. However, until adolescence the ab-

normality is subtle. During adolescence the normal pruning process goes haywire because of these abnormalities, and the subtle defects in the brain become greatly magnified. As a result, it is during adolescence that the symptoms of schizophrenia first appear.

[9] D. Jefferson, "Studying the Biology of Sexual Orientation Has Political Fallout," *Wall Street Journal*, August 12, 1993, p. 1.

[10] Maddox, "Is Homosexuality Hardwired?"

[11] M. A. Bozarth and R. A. Wise, "Toxicity Associated with Long-Term Intravenous Heroin and Cocaine Self-Administration in the Rat," *Journal of the American Medical Association* 254, no. 1 (1985); 81-83; M. W. Fischman, "Behavioral Pharmacology of Cocaine," *Journal of Clinical Psychiatry* 49, no. 1 (1988): 7-10 (Supplement).

[12] J. McDougall, "Identifications, Neoneeds, and Neosexualities," *International Journal of Psychoanalysis* 67, no. 1 (1986): 19-31.

[13] What about those homosexuals who are not promiscuous? A study of 156 male couples (performed by researchers, a psychiatrist and a psychologist who were themselves a male couple) revealed not one that had remained together and faithful for even five years. While "mere" infidelity of an indeterminate frequency may not be considered "promiscuity" by today's standards, it is clear that genuine monogamy is less typical of homosexuals than of heterosexuals, with few exceptions. Because in this study there were no exceptions, the researchers concluded approvingly that gay sexuality is inherently "nonmonogamous." D. McWhirter and A. Mattison, *The Male Couple: How Relationships Develop* (Englewood Cliffs, N.J.: Prentice-Hall, 1984).

[14] Some of the most advanced science of our era does indeed support the idea of such freedom. A discussion of this would take us beyond the scope of this book. See, for example, H. Stapp, *Mind, Matter, and Quantum Mechanics* (Berlin: Springer Verlag, 1994).

[15] *Midrash Rabbah* on Genesis 22:6, *in The Soncino Midrash Rabbah* (Brooklyn: Judaica Press, 1983). CD-ROM version © Davka Corporation and the Institute for Computers in Jewish Life (Chicago, 1992-1995).

[16] See especially *The Healing Presence* (1989) and *Restoring the Christian Soul Through Healing Prayer* (1991), both from Crossway Books (Wheaton, Ill.) and reissued in current editions by Baker Book House (Grand Rapids, Mich.).

[17] Bergner, *Setting Love in Order.* See especially the chapter entitled "Setting Love in Order: Disengaging Symbolic Confusion."

[18] Moses Chaim Luzzato, *Derech HaShem (The Way of God),* trans. A. Kaplan (Jerusalem: Feldheim, 1988), pp. 121-23. Unknown to the secular and Christian worlds, Luzzato (1707-1748) was one of the great geniuses of European Jewry. *Derech HaShem* is a brief but comprehensive summary of Jewish theology encompassing the Torah, the Prophets, the Talmud, and the Kabbalah.

[19] Remember, this is a more precise use of the word "profane" than in common usage where it frequently means "sinful." In some texts, the word "secular" is then used to characterize matters that are neither holy nor sinful.

[20] M. Nachmanides, *Iggeret HaKodesh (The Holy Letter),* ed. and trans. S. Cohen (New York: Ktav Publishing House, 1976), chap. 2; quoted in R. Bulka, *One Man, One Woman, One Lifetime* (LaFayette, LA:Huntington House, 1995), p. 137.

---

[21] See 1 Corinthians 10.

[22] L. W. Etheridge, *The Targum of Onkelos and Jonathan ben Uzziel on the Pentateuch with the Fragments of the Jerusalem Targum from the Chaldee* (Chicago: KTAV Publishing house, 1968), pp. 169-70; referenced in R. Frydland, *What the Rabbis Know About the Messiah* (Cincinnati: Messianic Publishing, 1993), p. 4. A "targum" is an interpretive translation from Hebrew into Aramaic. Since many of the Aramaic speakers in Israel at the time of the Second Temple and just after were not well educated, Aramaic translations generally fleshed out the text with extant understandings. A targum is much like an "Amplified Bible."

[23] This phrase, "the sinful mind" appears to be the English translation of the closest Greek approximation to the Hebrew *Yetzer HaRa*—the "evil inclination." The latter is an ancient Jewish expression found in the Talmud (recall that Paul was a Talmudic pupil of Gamaliel). The "wicked man" or the "evil man" is specifically defined as one who has allowed his *Yetzer HaRa* to overbalance his *Yetzer Tov*, or "good inclination."

[24] "And behold, a woman who had suffered from a hemorrhage for twelve years came up behind him and touched the fringe of his garment; for she said to herself, 'If I only touch his garment, I shall be made well.' Jesus turned, and seeing her he said, 'Take heart, daughter; your faith has made you well.' And instantly the woman was made well." (Matthew 9:20-22 RSV) Similarly: "And when the men of that place recognized him, they sent round to all that region and brought to him all that were sick, and besought him that they might only touch the fringe of his garment; and as many as touched it were made well" (Matthew 14:35-36).

[25] As explained earlier, in Hebrew the word for "fool" means not so much someone who is unintelligent in matters of the

mind as someone who is unintelligent in matters of the heart.

[26] Sigmund Freud, Totem and Taboo, standard edition (1913), p. 12.

[27] Michael Piazza, senior pastor at the Cathedral of Hope, commenting on Leviticus 18:22 and 20:13, which describe both male and female homosexuality as "an abomination" (*New York Times*, October 30, 1994, p. 16).